Things big, small, living, inanimate, natural, manufactured, beautiful, ugly, simple and complex.

photo
idea
index:

things

Things big, small, living, inanimate, natural, manufactured, beautiful, ugly, simple and complex.

photo idea index: **things**

JIM KRAUSE

HOW BOOKS

CINCINNATI, OHIO
www.howdesign.com

Photo Idea Index: Things. Copyright © 2009 by Jim Krause. Manufactured in China. All rights reserved. No other part of this book may be reproduced in any form or by any electronic or mechanical means including information storage and retrieval systems without permission in writing from the publisher, except by a reviewer, who may quote brief passages in a review. Published by HOW Books, an imprint of F+W Media, Inc., 4700 East Galbraith Road, Cincinnati, Ohio 45236. (800) 289-0963. First edition.

For more fine books for designers, visit www.howdesign.com.

13 12 11 10 09   5 4 3 2 1

Distributed in Canada by Fraser Direct
100 Armstrong Avenue
Georgetown, Ontario, Canada L7G 5S4
Tel: (905) 877-4411

Distributed in the U.K. and Europe by David & Charles
Brunel House, Newton Abbot, Devon, TQ12 4PU, England
Tel: (+44) 1626-323200, Fax: (+44) 1626-323319
E-mail: postmaster@davidandcharles.co.uk

Distributed in Australia by Capricorn Link
P.O. Box 704, Windsor, NSW 2756 Australia
Tel: (02) 4577-3555

Library of Congress Cataloging-in-Publication Data

Krause, Jim, 1962-
  Photo idea index. Things / Jim Krause.
     p. cm.
  ISBN 978-1-60061-044-8 (pbk. : alk. paper)
  1. Still-life photography. 2. Photographic composition. 3. Photography--Technique. 4. Example.
I. Title.
  TR656.5.K73 2009
  771--dc22   2009015544

Edited by Amy Schell
Designed by Jim Krause
Art directed by Grace Ring
Photography by Jim Krause
Production coordinated by Greg Nock

...another one dedicated to my son, Evan.

About the Author:

Jim Krause has worked as a designer/illustrator/
photographer in the Pacific Northwest since the 1980s.
He has produced award-winning work for clients large and small and is
the author and creator of nine other titles available from HOW Books:
*Idea Index, Layout Index, Color Index, Color Index 2,
Design Basics Index, Photo Idea Index, Photo Idea Index: Places,
Type Idea Index* and *Creative Sparks.*

WWW.JIMKRAUSEDESIGN.COM

Table of Contents

Introduction

"First of all, don't let the look of this book fool you. It's not a book of pictures. This is a book of ideas."

That's how the introduction to this volume's predecessor, ***Photo Idea Index: Places***, began. And, because it's a line that applies just as truthfully to ***Photo Idea Index: Things***, I'm repeating it here. These two books—as well as everything else I've had published up to this point—have this in common: they are *what if* books rather than *how to* books. In the case of the Photo Idea Index series, this means the images inside aren't meant as demonstrations of what I personally can do with a camera, but as suggestions of what you might want to try with yours.

Take, for example, this volume's first photo on pages 4 and 5. Yes, you could legitimately see it as a picture of light bulb. But I'd like to suggest that you view it as a brainstorming prompt that could lead to thoughts like, "*What if* I went around my house and tried to take some studio-quality shots of household objects?" or, "*What if* I bought some sheets of decorative paper from the art store and kept them on hand as backdrop material for all kinds of photos?" or, "*What if* I purchased a macro lens for my SLR so I could capture some really crisp photos of the intricate and tiny details of things around me?"

Don't take this emphasis on creativity and brainstorming to mean that this book contains no *how to* information. It does. Quite a bit, in fact. The last two pages of each chapter feature text related to that chapter's images. Sometimes the text conveys creativity-based ideas; sometimes it tells a story related to capturing that particular image; and sometimes it pertains to technical information regarding either the camera's settings or how the image was digitally processed in Photoshop.

And speaking of Photoshop, I mention its use liberally at the end of each chapter. Photoshop was my digital darkroom tool of choice for this book because I am a fan of its capabilities and functionality, and also because it's the most widely used image-processing software among photo professionals and hobbyists around the globe. If you've worked in Photoshop for any length of time, it's likely you'll be familiar with the adjustments, commands and filters I've used to treat this book's images. If you are unfamiliar with the Photoshop operations being mentioned, take heart: even the newest Photoshop users should be able to implement the featured treatments with a modest amount of hands-on practice (and possibly some consultation with the users' manual).

If you don't use Photoshop at all—or are a photographer who shoots with film—I believe you'll still find the digital effects mentioned in this book relevant: Most of the techniques described ahead can not only be mimicked by people who use other image-processing programs, they can also be replicated in the darkroom.

One more note about the digital side of things. Computers and software are ever-evolving. Some of the digital effects mentioned on these pages are sure to be updated, augmented or abolished at some point in time. As an example of what I'm talking about, a new version of Photoshop came out between the time this book was published and when its predecessor, **Photo Idea Index: Places** was released. The update included a treatment called the BLACK AND WHITE adjustment, and it proved to be a far more nifty way of converting photos to monochrome than what was available when I was working on the earlier book. (The method of monochrome conversion described in the earlier book still works, but the newer software makes the procedure far more efficient and versatile.) As far as the usefulness of this book is concerned, I'm not worried about these inevitable technological upgrades, and I don't think you need to be, either: The ideas presented here will remain valid regardless of changes in the means to pursue them.

No book is a cinch to put together, but for this one I really did enjoy snapping photos, digitally treating the results, and writing about it. Thank you for picking up a copy of **Photo Idea Index: Things**. I hope its content will confirm—and raise—the enthusiasm you feel for photographing the things around you.

1

*Extra*ordinary

Everything is photogenic. Every person, place and thing has something *extra*ordinary to offer a creative and resourceful photographer—it's usually just a matter of capturing the shot from the right viewpoint, in flattering light or in an intriguing context.

Things are the subjects-of-choice for this book. And here, in the opening chapter, the focus is on finding interesting and attractive ways of photographing particularly ordinary things—the kinds of objects you're likely to find around the house, office or neighborhood.

This book's images are presented without text. Technical information, anecdotal tidbits and project ideas related to each section's photos are contained in the last two pages of each chapter.

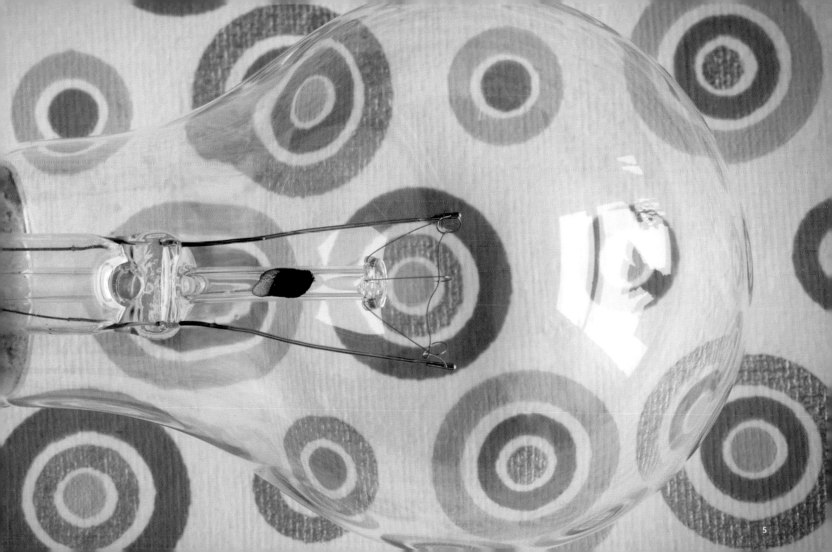

THANK YOU KINDLY
FOR NOT "DRAWING" ON
THE FOGGY WINDOWS - IT
LEAVES MARKS &

17

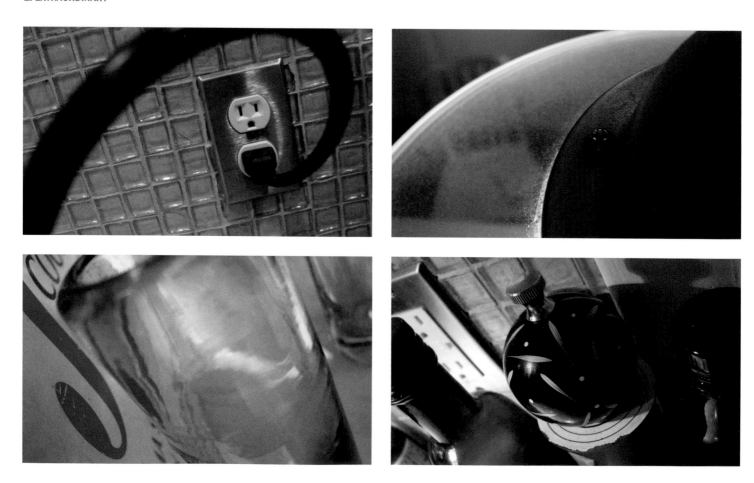

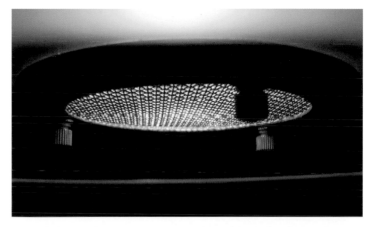

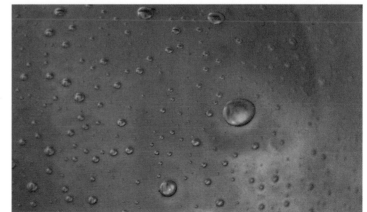

Pick up a light bulb. Look at it. It's a very ordinary thing, isn't it? Now, how about fetching a camera and spending an hour taking pictures of this unassuming subject of yours? Strive to shoot only photos that feel original and intriguing. How far can you take this? Will your hour of picture-taking turn into two? Three? You might be surprised how a simple creative exercise like this can boost your esteem for everyday objects *and* your range of photographic skills and approaches.

4
5

It's amazing what a backdrop can do. For example, consider the lively conveyances this light bulb has gained simply by being placed on a sheet of decorative art paper. I keep a large folder of assorted papers and fabrics behind a set of shelves in my studio: It's great to have these ready-to-go backdrops around when I want to spice up a photo.

If time allows, ponder the qualities of whatever it is you want to take a picture of—*before* you begin shooting. Look closely at the forms, features and textures that define your subject. Ask yourself, what are this thing's most interesting and descriptive attributes? Where should I place the camera in order to capture these details? Is the prevailing light adequate for a good shot, or will I need to do something to improve the scene's illumination? Can I place this thing in a certain setting to convey an intriguing message?

6
7

This spread, from left: the bulb's lit filament is shot with a 100mm macro lens; an end-view of the bulb, converted to a monochrome image using Photoshop's BLACK AND WHITE effect; the bulb's curved glass is used to warp the form of a nearby building; and the bulb after a makeover using a permanent marker and a scrap from the sheet of paper featured on the previous spread.

What about using Photoshop to convert your image(s) into a more graphic form of art? The flower-like design used for this page's background pattern was built by combining two views of the bulb's base. The illustration of the large bulb was created by applying a THRESHOLD adjustment to an ordinary photo of the bulb. Panels of pink and gold were painted into a layer beneath the bulb. The soft white fringe around the bulb was adding by using the OUTER GLOW effect.

8
9

I still had a couple shots planned for my light bulb when it was accidently knocked loose from its perch on a tall stand. This minor studio disaster turned out to be an opportunity in disguise (as minor studio disasters often do). The image on this page was created by photographing the bulb's remains and then adding a lit filament that was digitally borrowed from another image. Since the broken bulb emitted no light of its own, a small flashlight was aimed into the scene to create a pool of illumination.

Moving outdoors now... a trio of carved pumpkins share laughs (and a fright) on a porch rail. When you come across a ready-made scene like this, explore different vantage points from which to shoot—look for the ones that produce a likable composition and an agreeable interaction between the subject and its backdrop.

10
11

How about bringing some elements from the natural world inside for a photo session? This maple leaf was brought into my studio where it was clipped to a stand and lit with the narrow beam of a keychain light. The camera was set on a tripod since the low light conditions called for long exposures. A 100mm macro lens was used for the shot.

A set of old-school pinhole images—shot with a modern digital SLR. A pinhole lens was created by using a needle to poke a tiny hole in the SLR's removable dust cover (the cover that's unscrewed from the camera's body before attaching a regular lens). There are many different ways of using your SLR to take pinhole images—this is just one of them. My advice: Do an online search for the latest tips, techniques and photographic samples.

12   13

A tripod is usually needed to steady the camera when taking pictures through a pinhole lens (a typical pinhole exposure may last anywhere from 3 to 20 seconds). Digital SLRs take some of the guesswork out of determining correct exposure times for this type of shooting since they allow the photographer to review their shots and make adjustments according to what is seen on the LCD.

A willing and attractive model for your next photoshoot is only as far away as the produce section of your neighborhood grocery. What's more, vegetables and fruits rarely complain, are almost always available on short notice, and come in an amazing assortment of attractive shapes, sizes and skin tones. On this page, an artichoke poses boldly against a sheet of decorative art paper.

14   15

If you work as a graphic designer, you may have access to a camera you didn't even know about. That's right—the flatbed scanner you usually use to scan two-dimensional artwork, documents and photographic prints. Here, images of a halved onion and a trio of winter squashes have been captured by laying the subjects directly on the glass of an inexpensive scanner. (A cheaper model was used since I like the banded look of its imperfect images.) A cloth was laid on top of the onion and squashes to provide a backdrop.

As I write this book, I have an ongoing project in the works: to photograph every cup of coffee I brew or purchase for one year. The photos are snapped with little or no pre-planning, using a carry-along digital camera. The project is proving beneficial in more ways than I had anticipated: It's acting as a record of places I've been and things I've been up to from day to day; it gives my creative eye regular workouts (2+ times a day); and it serves as a reminder to keep a camera with me whenever I leave the house.

16   17

How about you? Do you have a daily routine you could turn into a creative workout? And what if you did begin a project such as this—what could you do with all your accumulated images? Some ideas: Compile the shots into a slide show or mini movie (complete with voice-over and/or musical soundtrack); display the images as a wall-filling home or gallery installation; insert the pictures into a scrapbook; or use the photos to fill the pages of a handmade book.

Interested in another creative exercise? Simply grab your camera and see how many different photos you can take within a confined space (a room, office or backyard, for instance) in an hour. The shots can be large-scale or close-ups, and the subjects can be shot realistically or as abstract impressions. Anything goes since the point of this exercise is simply to have a good time using the camera (neither stress nor overly high expectations are allowed) while stretching your creative instincts and technical abilities.

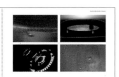

18   19

This type of picture-taking exercise is one of my favorites. Not only does it have all kinds of creative and skill-related benefits, it's also a lot of fun. Don't believe me? Give it a try the next time you're scratching your head over how to spend the next hour (or looking for a form of entertainment that doesn't involve the television or the Internet). The photos on this spread are from a set of images I snapped with simple digital camera over the course of an hour spent in my kitchen.

2

Collections

In spite of appearances, this isn't a chapter about doors and gates. The real purpose of this section is to promote the idea of capturing sets of related images, and also to demonstrate how broadly a collection's defining theme can be interpreted.

Photographic collections can be built around tangible subjects such as flowers, antique cars or cups of coffee. They can also be centered around abstract concepts like red, overhead, joyful or melancholy.

Got some collections in the works? If not, consider starting one (or several). Building collections is practical: sets of related images tend to be more appealing to galleries and stock-photo companies than portfolios of unrelated photos. Building collections is also good for a photographer's powers of observation, since it provides ongoing incentive to keep one's eyes open for potential subject matter.

Some gates have a kinder way of saying *keep out* than others. This ornate wrought iron fence outside a church in Siena, Italy, conveys its message and purpose far more eloquently than most. I collect images of doors and gates whenever I travel and wherever I go.

22

23

Interested in a few idea-starters for a collection of your own? Consider these: doors, gates, flowers, old tools, friends' shoes, friends' pets, hubcaps, crushed aluminum cans, empty bottles, mailboxes, chimneys, doghouses, window reflections, parking meters, garage sale signs, blurry people, hats, dumpsters, window planters, radio towers, junk food, mobile homes, numbers, letters or symbols. (See pages 256-273 for multiple examples of these last three items.)

Here, the solid rectangular form of a colorful door contrasts nicely with the fine and dark configuration of the gate before it. Photoshop's CURVES controls were used to heighten the contrast between the dark gate and the white wall. HUE/SATURATION adjustments were made to intensify the door's red hue while muting suggestions of any other colors in the scene.

24

25

When you travel to a foreign place, keep your eyes and mind open for the kinds of details that contribute to your visual and emotional perceptions of that place. I found the gilded and carved doorways to be just such defining detail during my month-long trip to Italy in 2007—along with swift mopeds, ancient cobbled streets, tiny cups of perfect espresso and spectacular public paintings and sculptures. I snapped dozens of photos of each during my visit.

In stark contrast with the ornate entrances on the previous spreads, serviceability is the theme that connects the doorways shown here. And, in keeping with the no-nonsense nature of the subjects pictured on these two pages, the images have been given a utilitarian treatment in Photoshop: The photos' colors have been desaturated using HUE/SATURATION controls, and their contrast has been beefed up with CURVES adjustments.

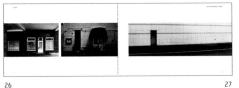

26

27

Not a lot going on in this photo, is there? Or is there? Minimalist artists might argue that the less you put into a composition, the more room there is for viewers' imaginations to roam.

Once they make their way through the opening of the skyward-facing exit/entrance at the top of the Guinigi Tower in Lucca, Italy, visitors find themselves on an observation deck high above the city, and in the surprising company of a group of well-rooted and flourishing trees.

28

29

It's difficult for any camera to properly expose all areas of a scene that contains both very dark and very bright areas. When shooting under these conditions, your best bet is usually to try for proper exposure in the scene's brighter portions, and to use Photoshop's SHADOW/HIGHLIGHT controls to bring sufficient detail back into the image's underexposed darker regions.

Whether you're collecting butterflies, stamps or photos of doorways, rare and outlandish specimens add to the value of your collection. I came across this set of oddly-configured doors just below the tower featured in the previous photo.

30

31

Being an American, I was drawn to the way in which the passage of time was conveyed through many of the aging doorways (and former doorways—as seen in this page's center image) I came across in Italian towns and cities. After all, I come from the Northwestern United States where the very oldest structures would be considered mere infants by European standards.

A locked and gated door limits access to a bricked-over railway tunnel between two towns of Italy's Cinque Terre. The image was originally shot in color, then converted to grayscale using Photoshop's BLACK-AND-WHITE controls. A CURVES adjustment layer was used to amplify the dramatic presence of the tangle of vines tracing the tunnel's arched entrance.

32

33

A wall of stones follows the terraced landscape of the coastal town of Vernazza, Italy. The painted blue doors in the wall lead to private overlooks above the similarly colored Mediterrenean Sea. HUE/SATURATION controls were used to boost the blue of the doors while simultaneously restraining the scene's other hues.

Open gates invite entry. This is true in real life—and also in photography where the image of an open gate or door can beckon a viewer's attention into a scene. Here, with its gate ajar, a wrought iron fence wraps around a group of turn-of-the-century grave markers in Charleston, South Carolina.

34

35

The geometric forms of a metal gate frame the view of a band of greenery between two tall buildings in Charleston's historic downtown district. This curious greenbelt is more than just a random congregation of plants—a shop owner from one of the adjacent buildings noticed my appreciation of the space and came outside to let me know it was under her personal care and supervision.

Doors of different sorts. Near page: A metal-clad hallway leads to a sturdy steel door inside an auto ferry. Opposite: A handpainted message at the entrance to a rural road has been painted onto a vintage truck's door. Both photos were shot using a 15mm fisheye lens.

36

37

If you are interested in presenting a collection of related images, think about coming up with an in-common way of treating the photos. For instance, convert all the images to black and white, tint each in a similar way, or show every photo with its hues richly saturated. (You'll notice this chapter's collected images of doors and gates have *not* been given an in-common treatment—this is simply because I wanted to present a wide variety of presentation options throughout its pages.)

3

Components

The purpose and personality of an evening gown, wristwatch or antique airplane are not only conveyed through their appearance as a whole, but also through the function and form of their individual components and details.

Try this: Wherever you are right now, look around and select an object. Now, ask yourself, *What are the components—small, medium and large—of this thing that best expresses its character, function and age? Which views of this thing might reveal its most aesthetically pleasing details?* How about applying this exercise every time you have the opportunity to consider a meaningful object's photographic offerings?

All the images in this chapter were shot during an afternoon spent in a single outstanding location: The Museum of Flight in Seattle, Washington.

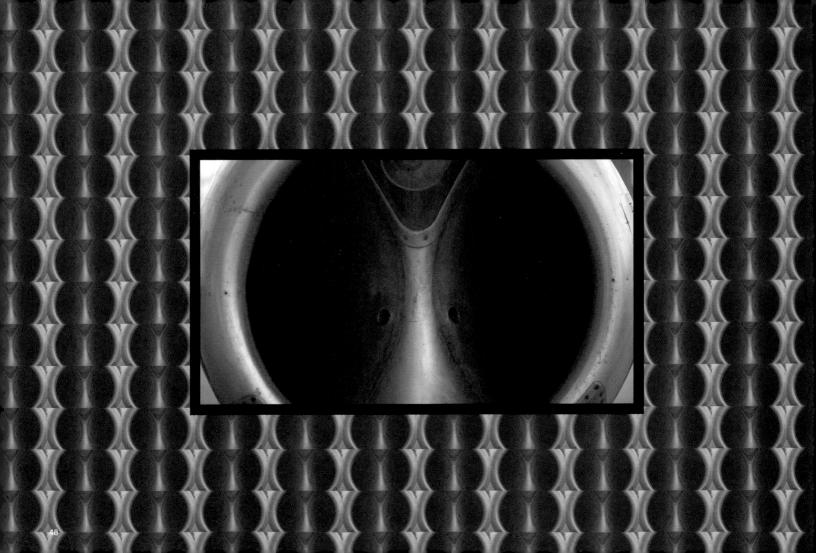

As mentioned in this chapter's introduction, all of the photos in this section were taken at The Museum of Flight in Seattle, Washington. My entire visit was spent focusing on the components of things, rather than on whole objects.

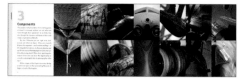

40

I took over 400 photos while at the museum (thank goodness for digital cameras and large media cards). This includes outtakes where I got the exposure or focus wrong, as well as unused shots from "brackets" (sets of three concurrently shot images where each image is exposed differently). Of my 400 or so images, I found 42 I wanted to save. That's a "keeper" rate of around 10%—about average for many photographers (including me... on a good day).

41

The pointy end. Wooden propeller blades, a steel-tipped spinner and a piston engine enclosed in sheets of hammered metal: This was the look of aviation in the 1930s. Fast-forward a mere forty years and you get the sleek, propeller-free design seen on the far page. It's hard to believe people only began flying in airplanes about a hundred years ago.

42

Each of the photos in this chapter was shot using a digital SLR fitted with either a 50mm or a 70-200mm telephoto lens. The pair worked beautifully as a team: I used the 50mm when I was able to stand near my subject, and I used the telephoto when I needed to zoom in from a distance. Both lenses were also able to capture shots with a pleasantly shallow depth-of-field.

43

Graphic designs. If whatever-it-is you're taking pictures of features typographic elements, consider spending some time photographing these graphic visual components. Not only do numbers, letters and symbols offer their share of aesthetic beauty to a scene, they also convey clues as to the purpose, age and cultural significance of the things they adorn.

44

Consider tinting your photo after it's been converted to black and white. Try out different colors and strengths of tint to find a result that best suits your subject. Explore your options using either the PHOTO FILTER effect or the controls available within the BLACK AND WHITE filter.

45

Available light. I spent most of my visit to the museum in its two main display areas. One is a windowless set of rooms, lit in the manner of an art gallery with overhead spotlights. The other is a large open space surrounded by tall walls of gridded glass. I used a tripod to steady the camera in the first section since light levels were low (I didn't want to use a flash since it would have overpowered the room's artful lighting). The second room offered more than enough natural illumination to make shooting easy and forgiving.

46

It's hard to go wrong when taking pictures of shiny airplanes on display in a room of glass and steel. Everywhere in this splendidly designed space, the surfaces of the aircraft were alive with light and reflection.

47

A hungry look. Whereas more recent jet planes mostly have pointed noses, the blunt front of this 1950s Russian MiG-15 is a wide-open air scoop (designed to satisfy its starved-for-air turbojet engine). How about creating a pattern out of a close-up such as this and using the pattern as a backdrop for the original image? That's exactly what has been done here. The background images have been lightened and tinted slightly in order to differentiate their appearance from the featured photo.

 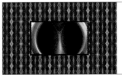

48

49

A face only an airplane fanatic could love. Landing and navigation lights lend notes of utilitarian personality to the DC-2 airliner on display outside the museum's entrance. Photoshop's HUE/SATURA-TION controls were employed to amplify what little color there was in the scene. When I use this control, I usually apply it as an adjustment layer and select "color" from that layer's pull-down menu. This helps limit the amount of unwanted digital noise that might otherwise be generated with the boost in color.

A 50mm fixed-focal-length lens was used to record this sumptu-ous melting-pot of light, reflection and form. "Fixed-focal-length" refers to lenses that cannot be zoomed (shots are framed by moving the camera rather than by turning a zoom-ring on the lens). The simple construction of these lenses—combined with their low light capabilities and extremely fine depth-of-field control—make them cherished favorites of many photographers.

50

51

The grayscale images in this chapter were originally shot in color. They were converted to grayscale using Photoshop's BLACK AND WHITE control. Each of the conversion options in the control's pull-down menu was considered before deciding which provided the most attractive result. The BLACK AND WHITE control is a powerful tool for converting color images to monochrome. It has far more flexibility than the simple GRAYSCALE command, and also allows a color tint to be added to the converted image.

Secondary subject matter. After taking pictures of an object's more descriptive components (things like wings, propellers and cockpits, in the case of airplanes) be sure to spend time focusing on your subject's less heralded details.

 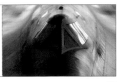

52

53

Here, the frame has been filled with the subject to create an image that's as much about aesthetics as it is about content. In this shot, a trio of studded space-age tires combine nicely as a monochromatic composition of curves, values and textures. Images that are based on simple tonal compositions are often equally interesting when viewed as a negative. What about pair-ing a positive and a negative version of a shot such as this and presenting the two together?

The two photos on this spread were shot using a 70-200mm telephoto lens. Many people think of telephoto lenses as tools for outdoor shots of wildlife, mountains and such. What they may not realize is that telephoto lenses have great value within the tighter confines of indoor spaces as well. For instance, a telephoto was zoomed in to capture this shot of a biplane's instrument panel from well outside the plane's protective rope barricade.

 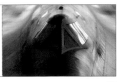

54

55

Here, too, a telephoto was employed to capture a shot that would have been impossible with a standard lens. In this case, the lens was zoomed from a balcony that stood many yards away from the subject. Note the intriguing impression of compressed distance that occurred when the telephoto was aimed along the plane's lengthy fuselage.

4

Close Up

An image that features a "close-up" view can be defined in a couple ways. For one type, the photo may be of a tiny object (or of a small detail within a larger object) shot from near the camera's lens. Another kind of close-up photo is where the scene being captured contains objects at varying distances from the lens, and is shot with the camera held very near something in the extreme foreground. Both definitions apply to the images ahead.

Most of the photos in this section were taken with either a carry-along camera set in macro mode, or an SLR fitted with a macro lens. A macro lens (or setting) does not necessarily magnify things, but it is capable of recording images that contain more detail than the eye is capable of seeing—images that can then be displayed at a size that allows for an even greater revelation of detail.

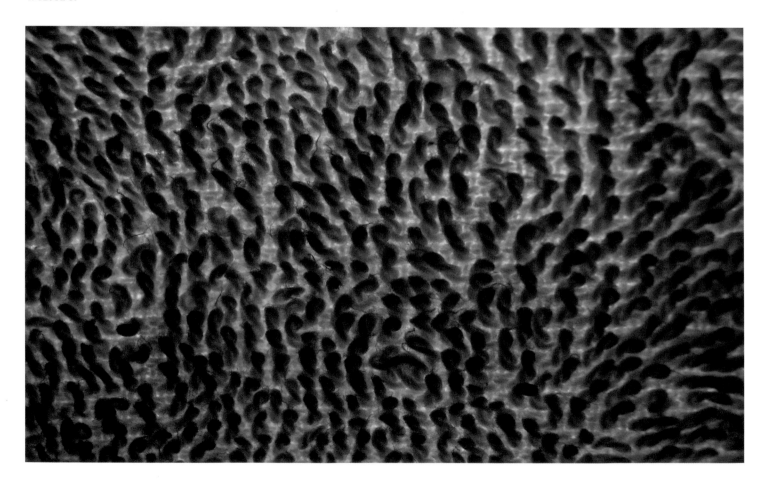

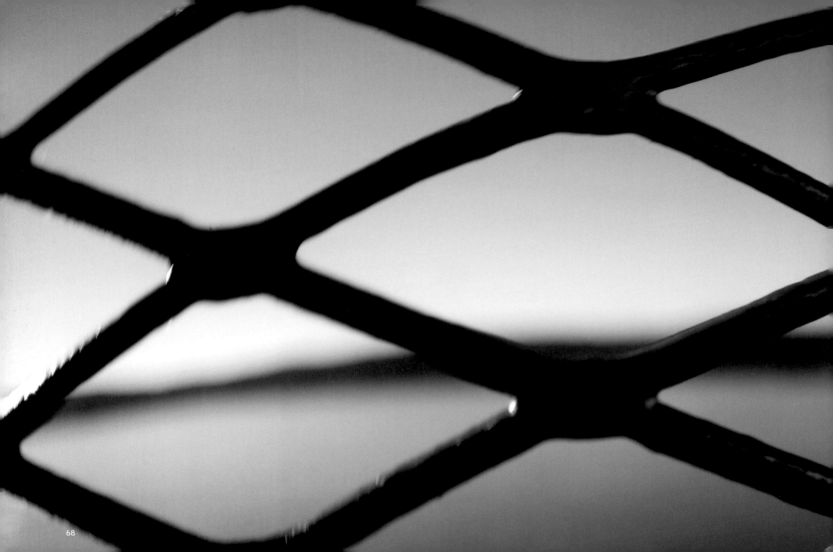

Frozen droplets of water adorn the metallic holiday ornaments hanging from a leafless tree. Originally, I got my camera out to photograph the entire tree, along with its decorations and a large portion of the front yard in which they were all situated. Once I started taking pictures, however, I found myself moving nearer and nearer to the tree and finding better and better shooting opportunities along the way. Finally, I decided the best shots were to be had from as close to the tree's ornaments as my lens could focus.

58

59

This image was taken with a 50mm lens attached to a digital SLR. A 50mm is a very versatile lens. Not only is it capable of capturing crisp close-up shots, it's also ideal for mid-range photos and portraits. Other bonuses of the 50mm lens: They are among the most affordable lenses available; they work exceptionally well in low light; they have extremely fine depth-of-field control; and they are very light and easy to pack.

Near and far. Impressions of space and distance can be amplified by focusing on something very near the lens while including far-away objects in the burred distance. Both of these images were shot using the macro setting on a pocket digital camera.

60

61

Aimed from just a few inches away from a sparkling, dew-covered mailbox, a 15mm fisheye lens has captured an interesting view of this rural sunrise. The photos on pages 66-69 were also shot in this manner using the same lens.

From the inside, looking out. Near page, left: Drops of condensation formed on the inside of a cafe window distort the view of a partially overcast sky. Right: A close-up perspective of an aging window frame and the soft-focus scene outside. Opposite page: Here, the camera has been focused on a dirty window pane in the extreme foreground while the view beyond has been allowed to melt into an impressionistic blur.

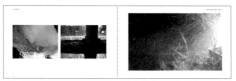

62

63

Most pocket and carry-along models of digital cameras offer a macro setting which allows the camera to focus on objects very near the lens (some cameras in this class can actually focus on objects *touching* the lens).

Household revelations. The macro setting on a pocket digital camera can reveal surprising new views of ordinary objects. The abstract visual on this page, for example, was captured by taking a picture of a towel from extremely close range using the macro setting on a pocket camera (the towel was lit from behind by draping it over the top of a lampshade).

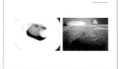

64

65

Left: An image of the inside of the coiled form of a fluorescent bulb. Right: The camera was set in macro mode and laid on a bare, quilted mattress to capture this view (a pillow and lamp can be seen in the "far" distance). Here's a simple project idea: Hunt around your home for an hour or two with your camera set in macro mode. It's very likely you'll be amazed at the photo opportunities that present themselves.

How about giving small objects—things that are normally photographed as tiny specks within larger scenes—a starring role in pictures of their own? On this spread, the featured subjects are a string of tiny holiday lights, a pair of salt and pepper shakers and a lone marble.

66

67

There was nothing special about the set up for this shot—it was simply snapped in the gameroom of a library on a sunny morning. I mention this to emphasize the notion that large collections of useful images can be built by people who keep a camera on hand while going about their daily business—even more easily, perhaps, than by a photographer who spends long hours working in the studio.

As you can imagine, the other camera-carrying passengers on board this ferry were aiming their cameras at the surrounding sights from *above* the level of the boat's waist-high guardrail. Not being in the mood to go along with the crowd, I snapped this photo by pressing a fisheye lens up against the safety fence's metal grid and taking a shot from there. If your goal is to capture a unique impression of a subject or scene, start by *not* doing what everyone else is doing with their cameras.

68

69

This photo, and the three that follow, were each shot with a 15mm fisheye lens. I enjoy the technique of aiming the fisheye from very near a foreground object while capturing sweeping views of the 'scapes in the distance. The artful, curving perspective of scenes shot in this manner (and the re-imagining of common views it creates), often amounts to photos that are both artistically attractive and visually intriguing.

More seaside fisheye views: each shot with things near to—and far from—the lens. Sometimes I'll spend a whole afternoon with a non-standard lens on my camera (usually a fisheye, a Lensbaby or even a pinhole). In a way, it's easier to take noteworthy photos with an alternative lens since the resulting images, if nothing else, stand a good chance of scoring points for originality.

70

71

As with all the monochrome images in this book, these photos were originally shot in color. This set was converted to grayscale using Photoshop's BLACK AND WHITE controls. In the case of these images, I felt the control's "high contrast red" setting made for the most dramatic conversions.

Insects, dead and alive. The scene on the near page was a lucky find. I had just finished taking the shot of the wood-framed window pane on page 62 when I noticed the corpse of this unlucky wasp in the corner of the sill. My carry-along camera's macro setting was used to capture the scene. The photo was converted to a tinted monochrome using the BLACK AND WHITE effect. A hint of color was added along portions of the image's edge with the PAINTBRUSH tool, set in "overlay" mode.

72

73

This colorful moth appeared on the ceiling of my house one evening. As soon as I saw it, I grabbed a step-stool, my SLR and a 100mm macro lens and took a few dozen portraits of the beautiful creature before carefully transporting it outdoors. A good quality macro lens can capture an uncanny amount of detail in tiny subjects—this moth was only slightly larger than a nickel.

5

Abstraction

Software makes it easy to explore far-flung visual interpretations of photographs. In this chapter, photos of ordinary scenes and objects have been converted into abstract compositions through the application of one or more basic Photoshop filters (for instance, the picture of an old truck's radiator, below, was transformed into the image at right using THRESHOLD and SOLID COLOR treatments). Each of this chapter's digitally altered photos are presented alongside their source images. Explanations of the treatments used to alter the originals are presented on pages 92-93.

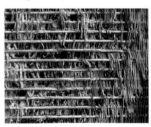

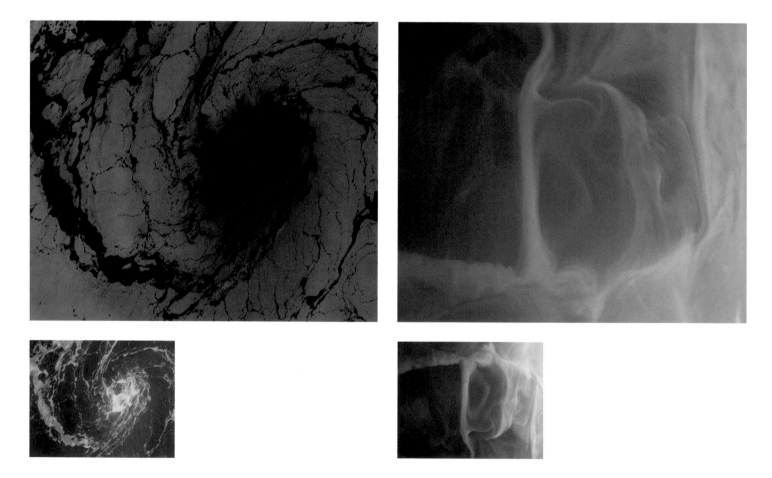

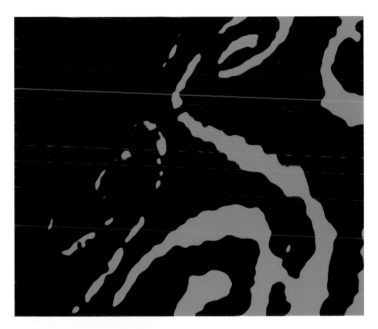

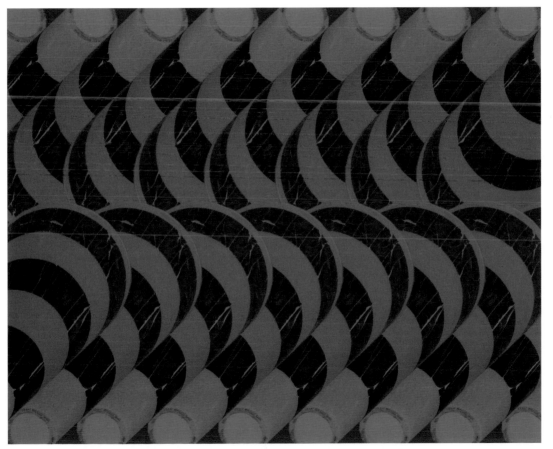

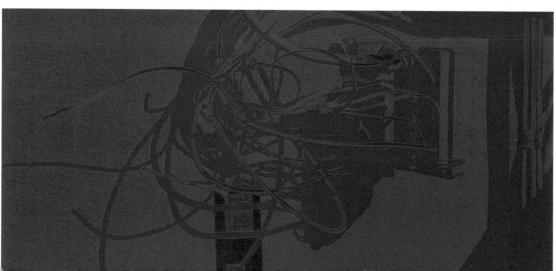

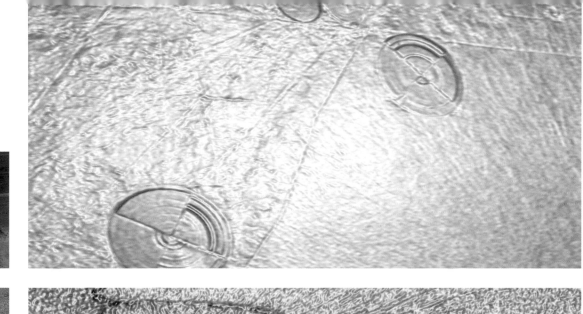

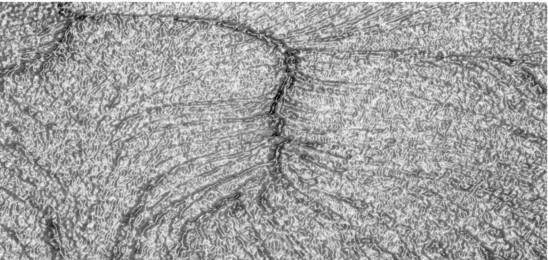

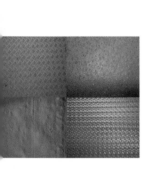

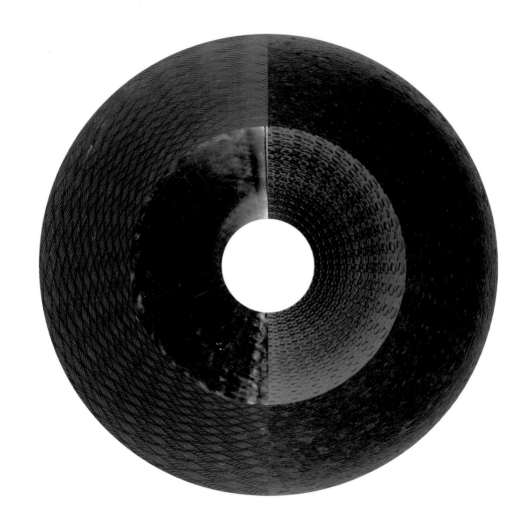

+

As promised on page 76, the original photos used to create this chapter's abstractions appear on these two pages. The original photos appear in the side columns along with production notes related to their alteration.

A Range Rover's radiator (right) was used to create the image on this chapter's opening spread. Photoshop's THRESHOLD command was employed to convert the original into a high contrast image. The result was colored with the SOLID COLOR effect.

Here, a photo of a grassy hillside has been converted into a painterly monochromatic composistion by applying BLACK AND WHITE and CURVES controls. The resulting image was duplicated and mirrored.

The ease with which Photoshop filters and effects can be applied, considered, saved or discarded makes exploration into fresh creative territory easy and quick. Hands-on experimentation such as this is also a great way to learn Photoshop (and more fun than reading the manual).

One photo of ocean foam, and another of milk cascading into coffee (as seen through the side of a clear mug) were treated with HUE/SATURATION controls to come up with this pair of moody abstractions.

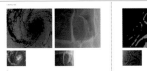

THRESHOLD and SOLID COLOR treatments have been applied to make dramatic changes to photos of

a piece of fabric and a wrought iron gate. Apply the threshold effect as an adjustment layer so that you can freely reconsider and readjust its effects until you are ready to finalize the image.

The WAVE filter and HUE/SATURATION adjustments were all that were needed to turn this photo of an ordinary airport tarmac into a colorful pop-art abstraction.

The form of a traffic cone was isolated using Photoshop's SELECTION tool, treated with the INVERT filter, colorized with HUE/SATURATION controls, and then cloned to create the pattern at left.

GRADIENT MAP adjustments were applied to these two photos to create the richly colored images at right. Investigate the outcomes that occur when using the GRADIENT MAP's ready-made palettes, as well as the effects that result when you input colors of your own.

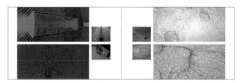

84   85

The PLASTIC WRAP filter was used to further amplify the abstract look of these two aerial   photos (one of farmland, the other of a snow-covered valley). Photoshop offers dozens of powerful image-altering filters and controls. Try them out!

A photograph of a swimming pool's cool steps were transformed into the smoldering composition at right by applying the INVERT command and a color-strenghtening CURVES adjustment. The image was also rotated 180°.

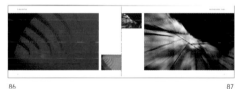

86   87

In this sample, a photo of tower-top scaffolding has been turned into a non-representational blur by applying the MOTION filter (set to "zoom"). The original image's palette was shifted with a HUE/SATURATION adjustment layer.

A composite image (built from four photos of metal surfaces) was treated with the POLAR COORDINATES filter to reshape it into the circular design at right. The design's colors were altered using the INVERT command and CURVES controls.

88   89

To create the ringed composition at left, a photo of a textured sheet of metal and the bronze door of an elevator were first joined, then treated to multiple applications of the ZIGZAG filter. The colors were re-tuned using HUE/SATURATION controls.

 +

Two photos (one of a granite wall and one of a glass vase's blue exterior) were layered together in different ways to create the four images on this spread. In the near sample, the layers were joined with the LIGHTEN mode between them. In the next image, the OVERLAY mode was selected.

90   91

In the third and fourth samples, the COLOR and DIFFERENCE modes were employed, respectively. Experiment with Photoshop's powerful layer modes when combining images. Also explore the changes that occur when you alter the stacking order of the images—as well as the level of opacity applied to each layer.

6

Water and Stone

Gary Larson, the creator of "The Far Side" cartoon, once drew a comic depicting an imagined moment in time when our human ancestry began in earnest. The cartoon features a fish-like, free-thinking primordial creature lifting itself from the water and sprinting over a stone with puffed cheeks (presumably filled with water) before submerging itself in safety once again.

Whether or not you believe the dawn of our ancestry looked anything like this, the humor in the scene is apparent, as is the widely held status of water and stone as essential ingredients of life-as-we-know-it. And whereas Mr. Larson paid respect to these natural elements using pen and paper, the goal of this chapter is to suggest ways of paying our own form of homage using the camera and pixels.

Sometimes you just have to get your clothes dirty when taking pictures. This shot was snapped with knees, elbows and sleeves in the wet sand and low surf (necessary to give my fisheye lens the view I wanted of waves rolling over a small beach rock). Since the waves were coming and going quickly, I put the camera in rapid-fire mode and took a string of pictures every time one rolled in. This gave me several dozen to choose from when the shooting was done.

94   95

I've never regretted purchasing a fisheye lens (15mm) for my digital SLR. It's a fun lens to use and I always enjoy looking through the viewfinder to see what kinds of crazy, curvy things it's doing with the scene before me. It was also a relatively inexpensive lens (only my 50mm and Lensbaby lenses were cheaper).

Water—drawn from air—condenses on the surface of a cold steel pipe. This intriguing example of visual texture was photographed in a public washroom using a pocket digital camera set in macro mode. The photo appears here after having its contrast boosted in Photoshop with CURVES controls. A red tint was added to the image using a PHOTO FILTER treatment.

96   97

Near page, left: A sideways view of a straw hovering in a clear plastic cup of carbonated water. A blue-green SOLID COLOR adjustment layer was added to the image. The opacity of this adjustment layer was set at 80% to allow a hint of the photo's original colors to show through. Right: A close-up of the bubbles atop a freshly poured cup of coffee. (This image was borrowed from my ongoing collection of coffee photos: see pages 16-17.)

A while back, I purchased a relatively inexpensive waterproof case for my pocket camera. It's been a useful gadget to have around. Sometimes I use it for underwater shots, but more often, I just use it to protect my camera when around water. This shot was taken by extending the camera into the spray of a shower head and snapping a picture using the camera's flash. Half the scene is dark because one of my fingers was accidently blocking part of the flash. No worries—I liked the nature of the composition that resulted.

98   99

In the previous photo, the action of moving water was frozen by using a flash. In this shot, the opposite approach has been taken: an SLR's manual settings were used to call for an exposure lasting several seconds. As a result, the streams of water pouring from this fountain have been transformed into soft blurs (same with the tops of the wind-blown trees in the background).

Ever notice how water sometimes looks wetter at some times than at others? Here's a photo that captures water in an exceptionally fluid-looking state. Shot from the low deck of a boat, on a morning where both sea and sky were subtle shades of mid-tone grays, I thought the dark silhouette of the sailboat in the distance provided just the accent needed to complete the scene. In the neighboring photo, stone, sand and sea meet along a beach near Santa Barbara, California.

100   101

Water as a mirror. A small fleet of rentable boats cast a rippled reflection from a deserted dock. This photo was taken from a low vantage point about 100 yards from the boats. A 200mm lens was used to zoom in on the scene. The morning fog—just beginning to lift when the shot was captured—did a nice job of muting the backdrop and allowing the foreground elements to stand out within the composition. Note the extreme horizontal cropping of the image. Ever crop photos of your own in this way?

A pair of images that each bring to mind the human spine: vertebrae of stone and water. One of my favorite things to do with my image cache is to look through it for photos that share conceptual or visual similarities—in spite of containing unrelated content. Chapter 13, Likenesses (pages 220-237), features several sets of connected pairs and sets of photos.

102   103

Giant monoliths of stone bask in the moonlight under the night sky in Joshua Tree National Park. This photo was taken in near darkness by placing the camera on a tripod and manually setting the exposure time for about two minutes (just enough time to transform the stars along the outer edges of the photo into short, curved arcs). The image was converted to grayscale and its contrast was significantly heightened using CURVES controls.

Left: A round rock lies wedged in a sandstone fissure. The egg-shaped stone offers pleasant compositional bonuses to the scene: it provides the image with a strong center of interest and serves as a visual hub to the numerous flowing lines that radiate toward its position. Right: Shadows reveal the contours of these well-worn boulders in Joshua Tree National Park. Photoshop's BLACK AND WHITE controls (set to "infrared") were used to convert the photo's original colors into a high-contrast palette of monochromatic hues.

104   105

This page, left: The physical texture of this slab of quarried marble was as attractive to my hand as its visual texture was to my eye. I came across this centuries-old specimen (about the size and thickness of a sturdy door) outside the Marble Museum in Carrera, Italy. The stone's intriguing finish was produced by countless strikes of a hand-pounded chisel. Right: More visual texture—this time the medium is the blue-green waters of the Mediterranean Sea.

This spread: cultured stone. In the left photo, a glimpse of warm sunlight and cool sea are framed beneath the arched stone entrance to a railway underpass. At right, water flows beneath the carved feet of gods, humans and animals into the massive basin of Rome's famous Trevi Fountain. The slanting shadows in the photo's foreground (cast by tourists) help the image's composition by directing the eye toward the fountain's central figures.

106   107

This page, left: An open-top storage room constructed entirely of piled rocks sits among vineyards in Italy's Cinque Terre. The photo was taken on a sunny afternoon and the foreground had to be underexposed in order to avoid overexposing the bright background and sky. SHADOW/HIGHLIGHT controls were used to bring detail back into the dark foreground. At right, an intricately carved stone column rises between panels of marble inlay on the exterior of a church in Pisa, Italy.

Reality vs. drama. The near image on this page has been printed as-shot. The photo is a realistic depiction of the scene as it appeared to my eye. In the image, opposite, true-to-life qualities of the original photo have been exchanged for a measure of drama: colors have been converted to a tinted monochromatic palette with Photoshop's BLACK AND WHITE controls, and its contrast has been heightened with CURVES adjustment layers.

108   109

Snapping a picture is only the beginning of a scene's journey from real life to photographic representation. As Ansel Adams once said, "You don't take a photograph, you make it."

7

Clouds

Few things have me reaching for my camera more quickly than the sight of an intriguing patchwork or blanket of clouds overhead. For one thing, clouds by themselves make superb candidates for photos. Clouds also perform wonders as scene-setters for photos of objects, landscapes and people. Whenever I find myself taking pictures under an interesting array of clouds, I immediately make it a priority to investigate vantage points that will include them in whatever scene I'm composing (this might mean kneeling or lying on the ground while shooting, switching to a wide angle lens, or both).

The two men on this raised platform were there to make a video of an upcoming demolition derby. Still, when I saw this scene, I suspected that a different story could be suggested if a photo were shot from just the right point of view. I had to smile when I took a look at the men from this vantage point—it suddenly appeared as though they were preparing for an interview with a fluffy white cloud or a soon-to-arrive celestial being.

112   113

This photo was taken from a seat about halfway up a grandstand next to the demolition derby arena. It was shot using a fully zoomed telephoto lens (70mm-200mm) with its aperture set at f18. This narrow aperture setting allowed the zoomed lens to record all the scene's elements in focus—thus minimizing the perception of distance between the men on the platform and the cloud with which they appear to be interacting.

A 12mm-24mm wide angle lens was aimed from the top of Giotto's tower in Florence to capture this panorama of city and sky. Wide-angle lenses have a wonderful tendency to create sweeping compositional convergences of clouds such as these—a convergence that visually funnels attention toward whatever earthbound subjects are in the scene.

114   115

A CURVES adjustment layer was selectively applied to the clouds in this image to deepen contrast and amplify their moody effect on the scene (an adjustment layer's effects can controlled by varying the opacity of its mask using painting and selection tools).

How about adding some textual or graphic elements to your images? Here, Photoshop has been used to layer a subtle pattern of asterisks into an overhead scene. Where else could you go with an idea like this? What kinds of symbols or words could you add to certain photos of your own? How about layering a poem or a short story over the top of a photographic image?

116   117

When interesting clouds are happening above, consider granting them compositional priority in your photos. In this image, the water-spouting creatures atop a Florentine fountain have been tucked into a corner of the frame—leaving the lion's share of the photo's territory to the sky above. The image's drama has been heightened with a strong application of CURVES and HUE/SATURATION adjustments.

Scene-makers. Notice the visual effects of the clouds in these images—how their forms point toward, connect and complement the structures below. The moral of the story: Pay attention to clouds and take advantage their generous aesthetic offerings whenever you can.

118   119

When shooting with a pocket camera, you can avoid overexposing the bright sky in a scene that also includes darker ground elements by following these steps: aim the camera toward the sky; press the shutter button halfway; keep the button thus pressed while you lower the camera's view; and then fully click the shot. This should eliminate overexposure in the sky (though it may result in a dark foreground—a condition you can treat with Photoshop's HIGHLIGHT/SHADOW controls).

Two of my favorite things in one scene: junk and clouds. I noticed this pile of scrap metal (including the hulk of an old Chevy that had been dragged out of the nearby sagebrush) on the infield of a racetrack in Spokane, Washington. What a photo opportunity! A side note: Take a look at the photo of this same car, featured on page 276. Amazing, isn't it, how a subject's presentation can be affected by shooting it from a different vantage point.

120   121

Consider your (lens) alternatives. Near page, left: This image was recorded by aiming a pocket digital camera through the viewfinder of an old Instamatic. Right: A Lensbaby was used to capture this impressionistic scene. The muted colors in the first photo—as well as the bright hues in the second—were generated using Photoshop's HUE/SATURATION controls.

So that's what the top of clouds look like. Be in the habit of reaching for a camera whenever you find yourself in a place that offers a novel view of an everyday person, place or thing. These shots, as you've probably guessed, were taken from the window seat of an airliner.

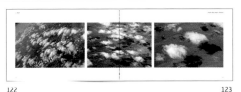

122   123

With a little help from Photoshop's image enhancement tools, you might be surprised how well a photo can turn out—even if it was shot with a pocket digital camera through the not-exactly-clear plexiglass window of an airplane. LEVELS, CURVES and BLACK AND WHITE controls were used to define these images' values, strengthen their contrast, and convert their palettes to monochrome.

A mirror, a window and a chrome-plated observation scope reflect the cloud-filled heavens above. Reflections, like shadows, often go unnoticed in daily life. Many of us have a tendency not to *see* these things—even when we're *looking* right at them. The good news is that the tendancy to overlook things like reflections and shadows can be overcome simply by applying a measure of conscious effort toward noticing them (especially when you have a camera in hand).

124   125

The limited palette in these three photos was created by adding a BLACK AND WHITE adjustment layer and selecting "screen" from the layer's pull-down menu. CURVES controls were then employed to fine tune the images' appearance. When applying this treatment, try out different settings within the BLACK AND WHITE effect's controls—a wide variety of results can be obtained.

Ever see clouds like the ones in the near image? I hadn't—not until one wet, windy and lucky afternoon last winter. The clouds only stayed in this form for a few minutes—just long enough for me to grab a camera and take a couple shots. Now that cameras are so readily available (even cell phones are taking halfway decent pictures, these days), we have never-before-dreamed-of abilities to share images of strange and rare happenings with people who were not lucky enough to be around when they occurred.

126   127

It's pretty easy to imagine a photo like the one in the middle of this spread appearing in a poster with an inspirational message, or as part of a brochure with a spiritually-inclined theme. And the clouds in the near image have even greater commercial potential—they could be used as a backdrop or filler for all kinds of advertisements and layouts. The point is, if you do any commercial design, save those cloud photos—they may prove useful one day.

8

Givers of Light

Everything we see—and photograph—appears to us courtesy of light. Light makes vision and photography (and *us*, for that matter) possible. Here, tribute is paid to the givers of light: the natural and fabricated entities that illuminate our existence.

Light reaches our camera in three ways: directly, indirectly and after being diffused. *Direct* light is that which travels straight from its source to the camera's lens without being significantly altered by the atmosphere in between. *Indirect* light reaches the camera after first bouncing off the surface of one or more objects. Light is *diffused* when it travels through a translucent material (or a not-quite transparent atmosphere) before reaching the camera. Examples of each of these incarnations of light can be seen in this section's photographs.

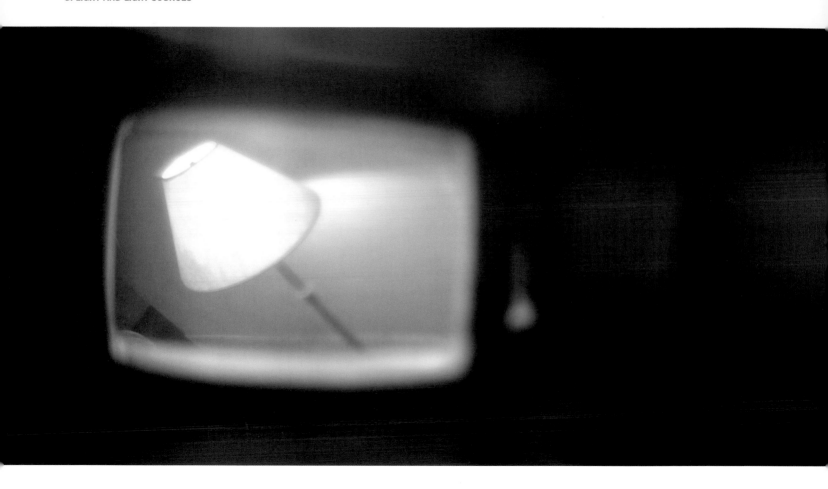

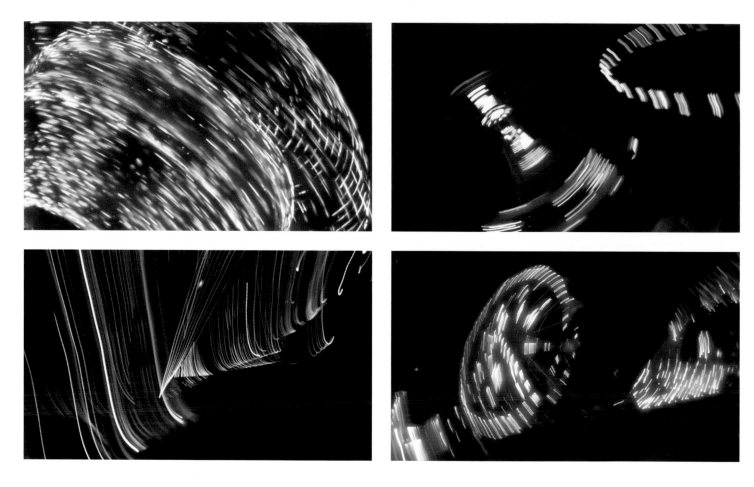

The bulb in a rustic light fixture comes to life as dusk settles over a colorful Italian courtyard. A certain amount of digital noise was generated in the image since it was taken in low light using a high ISO setting. It's often desirable to avoid this effect (common to film cameras as well), but don't automatically rule out shooting in conditions that generate a grainy image. Many subjects and scenes actually benefit from the earthy—almost tactile—conveyances generated by digital noise and film grain.

130   131

I had never seen this simple and charming style of municipal light fixture before my trip to Italy in 2007. Since they turned out to be the overhead-light-of-choice in most of the cities I visited—and since I also enjoy creating collections of related images—I decided to make a point of taking pictures of them wherever I went. The second spread in this chapter features eight more photos of this type of fixture and its near relatives.

A collection of related light fixtures from six Italian cities. Thinking in terms of collections helps remind me to keep my eyes open for photo opportunities when I'm traveling. Other improvised image collections I pursued during my month in Italy: sewer and drain covers, graffiti, words and symbols, signage, two-wheeled vehicles, doors, gates and windows. Got any collections of your own in the works? They're easy to begin: just take a picture of something you like and keep your eyes open for more of the same.

132   133

When presenting images in sets, consider digitally treating your shots in a way that establishes a clear visual connection between them. This spread provides an example of such a treatment. Each of its photos was desaturated in Photoshop with the BLACK AND WHITE effect, given a contrast heightening adjustment using CURVES controls, and tinted with a warming PHOTO FILTER effect.

Photos of ordinary things (such as the light bulbs and candle featured on this spread) often resonate favorably with people simply because of the familiar sense of connection the viewer feels with the image's content. In fact, many fine-arts photographers aim exclusively for photos of everyday objects and scenes. Commercially, too, photos of these kinds of things often find their way into magazines and websites devoted to topics such as poetry, writing and music.

134   135

I'm a fan of photos that reflect moments of simple pleasure in everyday life. The two images on this page were taken while sitting alone at streetside cafes. Both pictures illuminate pleasant memories of a particular time and place—in much the same way as an entry in a journal or a sketch in a notebook might do.

There seems to be a hint of interaction between the bulb in this scene and the painted face at lower right. Perhaps you'll agree that the on/off nature of light bulbs lends subtle conveyances of *being* to these inanimate subjects. In any case, when I took the shot, I felt the hanging bulb definitely added a more animated sense of interest to the scene than something like a drain pipe or an overhead beam would have offered.

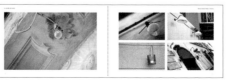

136   137

All color has been desaturated in these four photos, except for within the forms of the lights and lanterns featured in them. This color-restricting effect is easy to accomplish in Photoshop. Begin by adding a hue-cancelling BLACK AND WHITE adjustment layer over the base image. Once that's in place, use the LASSO tool to create openings in the adjustment layer's mask to allow color to show through in selected areas.

Looking for a lo-fi shooting technique? Try this: take a pocket digital camera and aim its lens through through the viewfinder of an older camera such as a Poloroid or Instamatic (generally available at second-hand stores). Experiment with different exposure, zoom and focus settings on the digital camera—as well as the distance maintained between its lens and the other camera's viewfinder—until you are satisfied with the level of clarity (or lack thereof) in your shots.

138　　　　　　　　　　　　　　　　　139

Here, two photos of the light fixtures in an antique store's upper story windows have been joined edge to edge. To add an extra degree of visual interest to the images, the reflections appearing on the window panes were amplified by using a CURVES adjustment layer.

An ominous sense of ambiguity permeates this shot of a steely lamppost and its gleaming cylindrical lights. The roiling sky above adds a feeling of unrest to the scene. The photo's contrast has been deepened significantly using Photoshop's CURVES controls. A heavy sepia tone was applied using the PHOTO FILTER effect. The NOISE > ADD NOISE filter was used to add a grainy texture to the image.

140　　　　　　　　　　　　　　　　　141

Mood-generating effects have also been applied to this otherwise pedestrian photo of a home and its front yard lamppost. To achieve this presentation, two CURVES adjustment layers were added to the original image: one to lighten certain portions of the image, and one to darken other areas. HUE/SATURATION controls were used to mute the photo's palette.

A chapter on light would hardly be complete without at least a couple references to the sun. In the left image, waves scatter the sun's late afternoon light in front of the hazy form of a distant island (this image was captured using the flexible focusing capabilities of a Lensbaby). In the right image, an intricate and structured abstraction is created by sunlight passing though the heavy glass bricks of a geometrically-designed skylight.

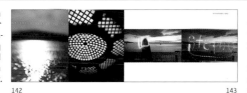

142　　　　　　　　　　　　　　　　　143

Here's something fun to try with your SLR. All you need is a darkness, light (from a flashlight, candle, etc.), a camera, a tripod and a friend. Put your camera on the tripod and set the exposure to about 15 seconds. Now, have your friend stand in the scene and move the light around. If they hold relatively still while moving the light, you might get an image similar to the one at left. If your helper moves about the scene while writing her name in the air, the camera will end up recording only the stationary scenery beyond (right image).

Night lights. Take your camera to the fair and be sure to stick around after the sun sets. Attach your camera to a tripod and experiment with lengthy exposure times. Try out different exposure and ISO settings and make adjustments to these settings based on what you see on your camera's LCD. To take photos of an even more abstract nature, remove the camera from the tripod and shake, rattle and wave it during long exposures.

144　　　　　　　　　　　　　　　　　145

Fairs and carnivals make excellent hunting grounds for photographers. Where else can you find such a rich assortment of irregular subject matter in such dense profusion (not least of which are the varied types and arrays of light fixtures)? Consider circling the dates on your calendar the next time you hear about a fair or carnival coming to town.

9

Shadow World

Shadows happen. All the time. Indoors, outdoors and in-between. But how many of us are really taking note of them—paying attention to the affect shadows have on the objects and scenes around us (as well as the fantastic assortment of shapes and forms of shadows themselves)? How much visual treasure are we overlooking and even trampling underfoot by ignoring shadows?

If you are interested in expanding your picture-taking repertoire beyond subject matter that is merely solid or has mass, consider making an effort to do what this chapter has done: pay special attention to shadows and grant them—at least some of the time—photographic priority over the people and things that cast them.

151

The ornate forms of a wrought iron gate are cast upon the marble walkway at the entrance to Rome's Monument to Vittorio Emanuele II. You know you're on track to capturing unique photos when you find yourself standing near a throng of photo-happy tourists and yours is the only camera aimed at the sidewalk.

148

149

Originally, the shadow areas of this image lacked any visible detail (the camera had sought to properly expose the photo based the brightness it was detecting in the sidewalk's sunlit areas). Photoshop's SHADOW/HIGHLIGHT controls were used to lessen the shadows' impact within the image and rescue the sidewalk's interesting textural contribution to the scene.

If "music is the silence between the notes," as Claude Debussy once said, then surely photography can be the absence of light. In photography, voids of light (a.k.a. shadows) have the amazing capability of describing objects to the viewer—whether or not those objects are even in the scene.

150

151

A plane and its shadow are about to reunite in Salt Lake City after parting ways in Seattle. I always request a window seat when traveling by plane, and usually spend a fair amount of time taking pictures once on board. (This photo and the strip of images on pages 122-123 were taken during the same flight.)

Background shadows can play strong roles in both a photo's composition and its projection of mood. Take a look at the dramatic interchange between dark and light in this shot of Cellini's famous statue of Perseus and the slain Medusa in Florence, Italy. (And speaking of drama, read up on Cellini's life story if you have an interest in over-the-top nonfiction tales of intrigue, passion, glory and gore.)

152

153

Rewarding photos can be shot when the subject matter is not necessarily viewed for what it *is*, but rather, as a *composition*. Midday light and deep shadows play key roles in transforming this relatively ordinary scene into a strong aesthetic display of lines, curves, lights, darks and textures.

Shadow figures. A group of racing cyclists is silhouetted under the lights at a nighttime event at the Marymoor Velodrome in Redmond, Washington.

154

155

I had to borrow a not-so-good telephoto lens for this event since my trusty Canon 70-200mm zoom lens was out on loan. The lens I had with me wasn't capable of taking in enough light for "proper" shots of the action. That being the case (and having no choice), I decided to use what I had and see what I could get. In the end, I was glad things worked out as they did. The impressionistic shots that resulted were probably at least as interesting as any technically "correct" shots I might have otherwise taken.

Timing is everything. These corner benches sat just below a flight of steps leading to the hostel I stayed in while visiting Italy's Cinque Terre. I must have walked past the seats a dozen or more times, camera in hand, without feeling any compulsion to take a picture. Then one day I arrived back at the hostel just before sunset and saw that a striking shadow had entered the scene. This time, I knew I was looking at a must-have photo opportunity.

156 157

This page, left: Evening sun casts a tree's long shadow over the form of a bricked-over doorway along a stone paved avenue. Right: Morning sun paints a diagonal sash against the textured wall of a tunnel leading to the circular central piazza in Lucca, Italy.

They call this *dappled* light—and it's definitely one of my favorite flavors of illumination. Here, the utilitarian surface of a metal water tower has been given a makeover through a painterly application of light and shadow.

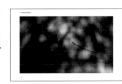

158 159

Leafy shadows embellish the stucco wall of an Italian villa. Both of the photos on this spread have been presented pretty much as-shot (the color was boosted slightly in each using HUE/SATURATION controls). This *au naturale* presentation seems to connect well with the simple content and moment-in-time quality of the scenes.

This spread, left and far right: While morning and evening light may cast the most interesting shadows in a horizontal scene, the downward slanting rays of afternoon sun can do the trick when it comes to upward-facing perspectives. In the near photo, a trio of elliptical shadows make an attractive extension of the metal hoops that cast them. In the far image, a stucco wall is decorated with the leaning forms of a window grate's slanting shadow.

160 161

Center photo: Like a sundial, a pillar's bold shadow extends through the ornate ring of a wrought iron enclosure and its decorative shadow. CURVES controls were used to emphasize the contrast between shadow and light in each of this spread's images. Additionally, a BLACK AND WHITE adjustment layer—with its pull-down menu set to "screen"—was used to mute the palette of hues appearing in each image.

Not wanting to wait for the bus, I walked from the train station at the edges of Assisi, Italy, to the historic city's hilltop center. A steep walk—and not short—but worthwhile since it led to a number of pleasant off-the-beaten-path discoveries. My favorite finding was this church courtyard of groomed gravel, pruned trees, covered walkways, stained glass and... a foosball table. The morning shadows lent just the right visual touch to the unexpected scene.

162 163

This sight reminded me of the egg tempera paintings of bicycles, people and shadows by the American artist Robert Vickrey. I highly recommend checking out a collection of this amazing artist's work. Much inspiration can be gained from the precision of his technique and his incredible understanding of light, shadow and composition.

10

Keeping It Fresh

The natural beauty, color, aroma and variety of flowers make them almost as irresistible to photographers as they are to bees. And because flowers have been so thoroughly photographed, by so many people, for so many years, anyone who now takes up a camera in hopes of capturing unique and original images of these wonderfully photogenic entities runs the risk of instead snapping pictures that appear unoriginal and stale.

Not to worry. Creativity (which, by definition, is the act of bringing something new into existence) can always be employed to find distinctive ways of picturing and presenting potentially overworked subject matter. The images in this chapter are offered as prompts of innovative ways to photograph—and digitally treat—images of anything that could benefit from a fresh approach.

A PHOTO FILTER adjustment layer (set to "sepia") was added to this image. "Screen" was then selected from the layer's pull-down menu. This treatment greatly enhanced the contrast between the scene's dark branches and light blossoms—and, at the same time, unified the photo's palette. A PHOTO FILTER adjustment layer can do much more than add subtle shades of color: Explore the effects that occur when its pull-down menu is set to different options.

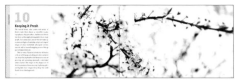

166

167

It's okay to bring an image into Photoshop with only a loose idea of what you want to accomplish. Jump right in and experiment with the effects of different filters, controls and commands. Save promising outcomes along the way and keep at it until you find a treatment (or a combination of several) you like. Not only does this type of not-by-the-book exploration lead to unexpected and attractive outcomes, it's also an excellent way to expand your knowledge of how Photoshop works and what this amazing program can do.

Here's an idea: Go to a florist, buy some flowers, bring them home and take some pictures. And while you're at it, spend time concentrating on the smaller features of your subjects—the individual elements that add up to the whole. A 100mm macro lens was used to crisply capture a sunflower's finer details in this page's images. If you don't have an SLR and a macro lens, how about a pocket digital camera? You might be surprised at how well a modern pocket camera can handle close-up work.

168

169

And what about taking pictures of flowers before they bloom (or long after, as seen in this chapter's final spread)? The set-up for this scene was quite simple: the subject's stems were steadied and held in place using bulldog clips; a sheet of black matte board was placed in the background; the blinds of a nearby window were raised to provide illumination; and a sheet of white paper was placed to the left of the frame to reflect additional light onto the buds. The shot was taken with a 50mm lens.

A sheet of decorative tissue paper was hung between this flower and a bright desk lamp. Not wanting the flower to appear completely in silhouette, I added a few highlights to its petals by aiming a small key-chain light from above.

170

171

After shooting the image, opposite, I moved the flower so it was behind the translucent sheet of paper, but still in front of the lamp. I then manually focused the camera on the flower (auto focus would have insisted on seeing only the sheet of paper nearest the camera's lens) and opened the lens' aperture wide to establish a shallow depth-of-field. I experimented with several aperture settings before deciding on one that created just the right degree of abstraction from the paper's ornamentation.

Ever seen the blooms of a hoya plant? Each intricate, puffy, star-like flower is about the size of a pea. Here, a group of these tiny blossoms float comfortably in a canning jar that would hardly be large enough to support the stems of a more traditional bouquet. Surprise and educate your friends with your photos of unusual botanical specimens such as these.

172

173

Sometimes beauty has to be ignored in order to find attractive photo opportunities. Near page, left: The colorful blooms at the top of these stems prompted me to pull out my camera, but it was the sense that the world already had enough of photos of pretty blossoms that caused me to concentrate on the watery composition of glass, liquid and stems below. Do you ever hear a tiny voice telling you to look further before taking a shot? If so, listen.

Though they occupy only a small portion of this photo's territory, the presence of the flowers in this hillside shrine has been amplified by muting hues elsewhere in the scene. This effect was accomplished by adding a BLACK AND WHITE adjustment layer to turn the entire image to monochrome. The PAINTBRUSH tool was then used to airbrush a soft-edged hole through the color-canceling adjustment layer.

174

175

A solitary sunflower, as seen through a pinhole lens. (Check out pages 12-13—and the Internet—for more information about taking pinhole shots with your digital SLR.) What do you think about the large amount of black space included in this shot's composition? Ever try recording and presenting an image of your own in a similar way?

This was a lucky shot in that I just happened to notice—the night before it was taken—that the empty space beneath the blossoms on these cherry trees resembled the shape of a VW bug. Lucky, too, in that I had a friend willing to drive her VW into town the next morning so I could snap some photos.

176

177

Here, Photoshop has been used to give the image an additional infusion of flower power: The car's exterior has been overlaid with blossoms borrowed from another image. This was done by first selecting the VW's form using the LASSO tool, and then pasting another image's flowers into the selection area. The new flowers were pasted into a layer of their own, and its pull-down menu was set to "soft light."

How about using Photoshop to add a typographic message to your image? Here, a selection made from the letterforms of the word "bloom" have been used to selectively apply the effects of a HUE/SATURATION adjustment layer. The HUE/SATURATION layer's controls were set to create a desaturated, "colorized" version of the original photo wherever its effects were applied.

178

179

As for the underlying image itself, this was a simple snapshot taken with a pocket digital camera during an outdoor coffee break. Before cloning and mirroring the image, its colors and contrasts were amplified using CURVES and HUE/SATURATION controls.

The next time you have some flowers around the home or office, how about keeping them on hand until they are long past their prime, and then taking some pictures? The sunflower in this spread's near image is the same as was featured on page 168. The flower in the adjacent image is the same as was used for the pair of photos on pages 170-171. Both of these flowers were kept on a back shelf in my studio for three months after their first photo session before these shots were taken.

180

181

This photo was taken using a 100mm macro lens with its aperture set very narrow (f22). This resulted in an image where the dead flower—and the painted background behind it—were both in sharp focus. Photoshop's BLUR tool was used to soften the focus around the photo's perimeter as a way of allowing the crisp form of the flower to stand out decisively within the scene. The image's perimeter was also darkened slightly using the DISTORT › LENS CORRECTION › VIGNETTE effect.

11

Flora and Forest

The plant kingdom is the focus of this chapter; living creatures are featured in the next. Admittedly, the photos on the next thirty-four pages do little to catalog the staggering breadth of variety found in either of these categories. (Did you know there are believed to be at least 80,000 species of plants in the Amazon basin alone, and upwards of half-a-million types of beetles worldwide?)

Still, cataloging isn't the aim here—but rather, the lending of ideas that could be applied to your photographs of the world's flora and fauna.

The photos on the pages ahead reveal my own favoritism toward trees and forest plants (I've lived in the Northwest corner of the U.S. most of my life). Apply whatever picture-taking ideas that come to mind when viewing these images to the kinds of plants you live near and enjoy.

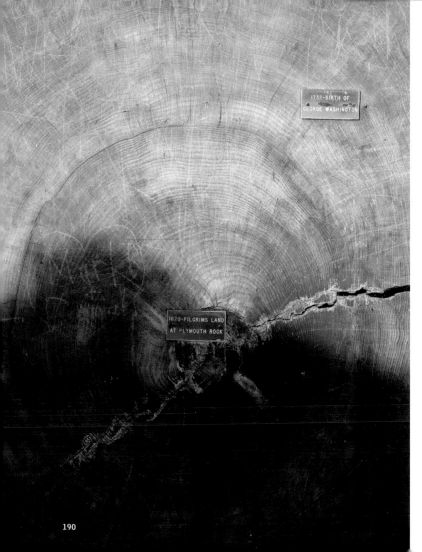

1732-BIRTH OF
GEORGE WASHINGTON

1620-PILGRIMS LAND
AT PLYMOUTH ROCK

American False Hellebore, American White Hellebore, Bear Corn, Big Hellebore, Corn Lily, Devil's Bite, Duck Retten, Indian Hellebore, Itch-weed, Itchweed, Poor Annie, Blue Hellebore, or Tickleweed. Regardless of what you choose to call these beautiful low-alpine plants, their broad and precisely ridged leaves make excellent photographic subjects—especially when they are painted with a soft scattering of filtered afternoon sun.

184   185

Nature offers an abundance of scenes that are big on visual texture (defined here as an image with a lot going on, but no clear center of interest). Photos that are rich in attractive visual texture not only make good stand-alone images, they can also be used commercially for things like backdrops behind an advertisement's headline, a theme-setting image on a brochure cover, a website's masthead or as wall-cover behind a sales display.

This free-floating image was created by using Photoshop's LASSO tool to select a plant's outline from within its original image. Once the selection was made, it was feathered slightly, copied, and pasted over a white background in a fresh document. It takes practice to be able to accurately select complex forms using the LASSO tool. I prefer to zoom in on the subject and use the tool's "polygon lasso tool" option to create selections from a series of closely-spaced dot-to-dot clicks of the mouse.

186   187

Interested in the planet's flora? How about starting a collection of photographic specimens? Approach your subjects in the manner of early botanists who recorded personal impressions with sketch pads, pencils and paint. Like the work of many of these inquisitive and creative women and men, your own images could reflect a blend of intellectual interest and artistic expression.

Medium, big and small. Be sure to consider views and subject matter of all three types when you're out taking pictures in a plant-filled place. From left to right, the lenses used for this spread's photos were: a standard zoom (24-70mm); a wide angle (12-24mm); and a macro (100mm).

188   189

When I'm able to bring multiple lenses with me outdoors, I try to match my eye's vision with whatever lens is currently fixed to the camera. For example, I might begin the outing using a wide angle lens and looking for large landscape views. Then I'll switch to a standard zoom lens and look for more tightly framed scenes and medium-sized details (many of which I might have noticed during the search for larger panoramas). And finally, I'll attach a 50mm lens, or even a 100mm macro, and go after some close-ups.

Near page, clockwise from left: A cross-section of a giant Douglas fir reveals the fantastic age it reached before being converted to lumber; a grove of olive trees—their trunks connected by colorful fruit-catching nets that have been twisted shut for the winter; a gaggle of tall palms reaching for the sky (the BLACK AND WHITE filter's "infrared" setting was used to convert this scene to monochrome).

190   191

A Joshua Tree—charred during a recent brush fire—continues to broil under the afternoon sun in Joshua Tree National Park (summer temperatures in the park regularly soar above 110°F). The bleakness of the panorama was emphasized by converting the colors in the foreground to a palette of chalky hues. This was accomplished by adding a BLACK AND WHITE adjustment layer with its pull-down menu set to "screen." CURVES controls were used to boost contrast within the image.

Nature rarely makes a misstep in terms of aesthetics. Here, snow and a tree's limbs combine to offer the camera an intricate fractal composition of lines, curves and values. To maximize the presentation of this scene's aesthetics, the photo was converted to grayscale (which wasn't a stretch, since it had little color to begin with) and given a contrast-enhancing treatment using Photoshop's CURVES controls.

192   193

Here, a photo of towering trees has been converted to grayscale and inverted (made into a negative)—a good example of simple effects being applied to significantly alter a shot's presentation and impact.

Photographed from the top of the Guinigi Tower in Lucca, Italy, the mini-arboretum in the near image sits neatly framed by the sea of red tile rooftops surrounding it. Visual framing was also the key to the second image's composition—pillars and an arch set the scene for a pair of trees in an Italian courtyard (I was standing just a few feet from the foosball table featured on page 162 when I took this shot).

194   195

Near page, left: I thought I'd found someone's missing bonsai plant when I chanced upon this tiny sapling rising from the base of a long-gone lamppost. Right: A scraggly weed fights its way up from a crack in a sidewalk—only to find itself in the confines of a steel cage. (A powerful metaphor for hopeless persistence? A hopeful metaphor for the power of persistence?)

A tree, alone with its reflection, stands watch over the fog-enshrouded waters of Cascade Lake on Orcas Island in Washington state. I tried out several different ways of framing the scene before deciding the views I liked best were the ones that contained the least.

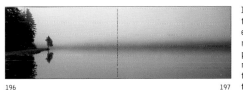

196   197

I passed this scene while on my way from one end of the island to the other (I wasn't in picture-taking mode, but I did have my camera with me). Anyway, like I said, I *passed* the scene initially—drove right by it knowing full well I should have pulled over to take some pictures. Eventually, guilt and my creative instincts got the better of me and I turned the car around and took some photos. I can't say the forces of creativity always win in my personal battles against the forces of routine, but I'm working on it. How about you?

I came across a scattering of these prickly seed pods while on a lunchtime walk beneath a row of deciduous trees. Fascinated by the appearance and structure of the pods, I stuck a few in my coat pocket and brought them back to my studio for a photo session. How about bringing a bit a nature back with you the next time you come across some interesting specimens in the wild?

198   199

These scenes have been *painted with light*. Painting with light is a technique where the subject is placed in an unlit (or barely lit) space; the camera is put on a tripod and set for a long exposure (anywhere from 5 to 30 seconds); and a handheld light is freely moved around the subject while the camera is exposing the shot. Every image comes out differently with this kind of free-flowing illumination technique. Use the camera's LCD to check outcomes as you work, and make adjustments accordingly.

12

Creatures

Let me make one thing clear: I'm not a wildlife photographer. I've never been scuba diving, never gone on safari, and have never spent a week in a bird-blind stalking waterfowl with a telephoto lens. I'm just a person who enjoys an occasional hike, afternoons at public aquariums, and hanging around with friends' pets. So keep in mind, when you're looking at the photos in this section, that the images featured here were shot by a person with modest photographic equipment, a reasonable attraction toward animals, and an aversion to the suffering a true wildlife photographer has to regularly endure to make their living.

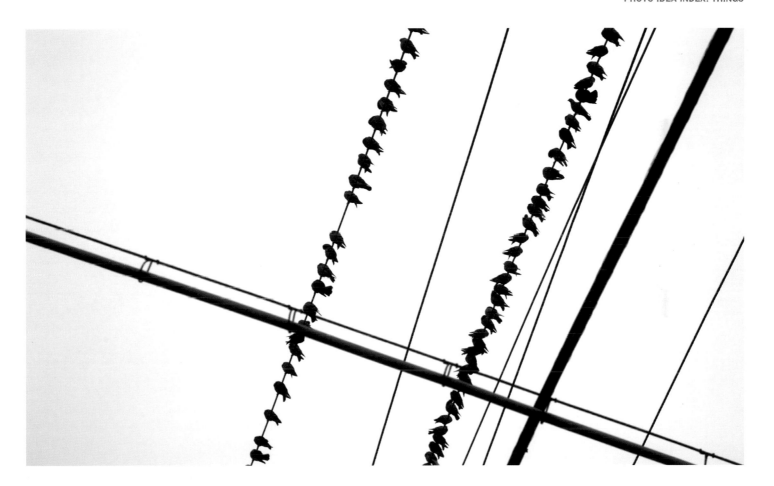

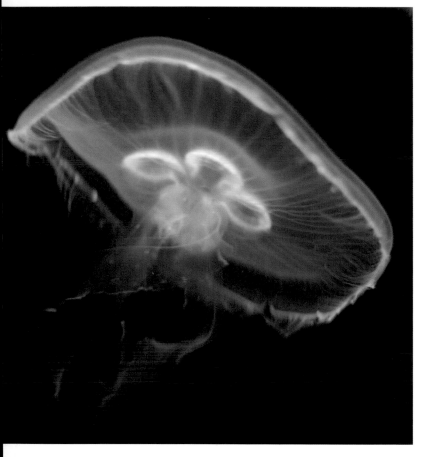

Crocodiles of Belize: *Belize is host to two species of crocodile: The populous* AMERICAN CROCODILE *and the less common* MORELET'S CROCODILE. *American crocodiles range throughout Central America and the Caribbean islands and live mostly in coastal habitats such as mangrove forests and the mouths of rivers (both saltwater and fresh). Morelet's crocodiles mainly inhabit the freshwater environments of inland Belize—marshes, lagoons, and slow moving rivers. Morelet's crocodiles are about half the size of American crocodiles. Neither species is considered overtly predatory toward humans but both represent a potential threat should be treated with utmost respect and caution.*

As pointed out in this chapter's introduction, the photos on these pages are those of a non-card-carrying wildlife photographer. Most of the creatures inhabiting the pages ahead were photographed while I was either out walking, taking pictures of other things, visiting at a friend's house or spending an afternoon at a place like an aquarium or zoo (where barriers of glass, metal and wood keep the animals and humans conveniently separated).

202   203

Not being thrilled with the look of the colors in this image's original version, I decided to explore my grayscale and tinting options using Photoshop's BLACK AND WHITE controls. When you come across a photo in your collection—a photo you like, but aren't quite sure how to make the most of—that's as good a time as any to start exploring alternative avenues of presentation using digital filters, adjustments and effects.

Clockwise, from top left: A pigeon takes off from its towering perch above the red tile roofs of Lucca, Italy; wind-blown palms share the scene with pair of pelicans riding seaside currents of air in Hopkins, Belize; a neat line of Canadian geese paddle the waters off the shore of Orcas Island in Washington state; and a murder of crows (believe it or not, that's the terminology used to describe a group of crows) hangs out in the branches over a sidewalk in my hometown of Bellingham, Washington.

204   205

A congregation of roosting pigeons adds pleasing notes of variation and interest to this tidy linear composition of overhead power lines. Use the viewfinder to explore various camera angles and orientations before you snap a photo of a scene as graphically structured as this one. Try to make the most of the spacial relationships being offered.

Easy as shooting fish in a barrel—only this time the shooting was done with a camera, and the barrel was a public aquarium. If I hadn't told you the the photos on this page were taken while keeping my feet dry, would you have guessed? Scuba gear and watertight camera cases—as it turns out—are not *required* equipment when it comes to taking pictures of exotic undersea creatures.

206   207

Who's on display here, the fish inside the tank or the tourists outside? In this photo, the natural light from a nearby wall of windows reflects against the thick transparent exterior of a jumbo fish tank at the beautiful public aquarium in Charleston, South Carolina.

I photographed this gnarly crocodile from behind a safety fence at a preserve near Hopkins, Belize. The croc's portrait was lifted from its original image using Photoshop's LASSO tool. After the selection was made, its edges were feathered slightly before being cut-and-pasted onto a white background. The subtle shadow beneath the creature was added using the PAINTBRUSH tool.

208   209

It's not too tough to take a picture of an animal whose first line of defense is to hold very, very still. This lizard was kind enough to stay put from the moment I saw it until I'd had a chance to snap its portrait. Still, it was a one-shot deal: the tiny creature darted off as soon as it heard the click of the camera's shutter.

Separated at birth? The beaming lens of an overhead track light and a sunflower's center bear strong visual similarities. How about looking for pairs of visually and conceptually related photos in your own image cache? A couple dozen such pairs might make for an interesting web-posted collection or gallery showing.

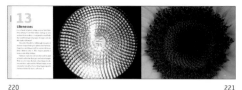

220   221

The fine detail in these two close-up images was recorded with a 100mm macro lens. If you have an interest in capturing exquisitely detailed images of small objects, consider adding a macro to your collection of lenses.

Unlike the undersea creatures featured on pages 206-207, the Cannonball jellyfish shown on this page is a wild specimen (its portrait was taken using a pocket camera housed in a waterproof case). Here, the jellyfish's form has been paired with an unlikely visual relative—the burning range-top element of a gas stove.

222   223

Near page, left: the partially peeled remains of a handbill in a window. To the right, a trio of utility covers. These two images come from folder in my hard drive entitled, *Looks-Like-a-Face*. The folder receives new material regularly.

Shared visual characteristics connect most of the pairs and sets of images in this chapter. By contrast, the bond that links this foursome of photos is mainly thematic: *Captivity*.

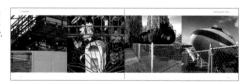

224   225

From left: A hand from Bernini's spectacular sculpture in Italy's Piazza Navona reaches for help from inside a construction barricade; Betty Boop bides her time with other antiques behind the ornate bars of a wrought iron fence; a retired steam engine sits at the end of its track inside a chain-link enclosure; and a fenced-in jetliner sticks its nose over a locked gate (this image would also have made a nice companion to the photo of the attention-seeking dog on page 213).

Here, the ribs of an old-fashioned metal heater complement the look of the damp palm fronds in the adjacent photo. The colors in the two images are complementary as well.

226   227

Like a pair of lovesick snails, two large mechanical devices (about the size of washing machines) sit near a pile of industrial junk at a wrecking site. In the adjoining image, an insect couple lounges on a warm hunk of rusting metal. The first photo was shot from a considerable distance using a fully zoomed telephoto lens. The second photo was snapped using the macro setting on a pocket camera—the subjects were just an inch or so from the lens.

S-shaped swirls connect the content of this spread's photos. From left: a fence ornament, frosted with snow from an overnight flurry; a pair of window-shutter brackets, dappled with afternoon light; and the logo on a bicycle seat, dampened with morning dew.

228　229

Connected through their content, the members in this trio of images also convey notes of individuality—thanks in part to the different colors that have been used to tint each image. The tints were applied using the versatile set of adjustments available within Photoshop's BLACK AND WHITE effect.

I came across this lip-like bloom (lower image) while hiking in a jungle preserve in Belize. Even as I was taking the photo, I knew it was destined to end up in my collection of likenesses—all I needed to do was locate up a pair of good-looking human lips and snap their portrait.

230　231

In some cases, the visual or thematic link between this chapter's photos is obvious. In other instances, the connection is more obscure. If you were to create a series of likenesses from images of your own, how apparent would you want the relationships between them to be?

From left: A bucket serves as an improvised ashtray for an outdoor wedding; the round "O" of a tire swing hangs above the elliptical form of its shadow; a makeshift coin-toss game—painted onto a floating deck next to a ferry landing—collects extra income for the resourceful dock-workers who crafted it; and a frosty donut of snow sits on top of municipal garbage can.

232　233

If you'd been the one to come across the scene of soggy cigarette butts pictured at far left, would you have taken a shot? Now, I'm not saying you wouldn't have—or that I'm special because I did—I only mention it because it brings up a point: If a photo of something as non-spectacular as this can someday make it into a personal collection (as well as onto the page of published book), what's to stop any of us from taking and saving photographs of anything and everything that calls to us for attention?

A couple tips for viewers who are feeling inclined to search their own image cache for pairs and sets of likenesses: Keep an open mind—there's no way to know ahead of time what kinds of associations will arise as you look through your photos; and, when you come across an intriguing solo image, move it to an "on hold" folder where it can be easily found if/when a photo that shares some of its qualities is found.

234　235

It wasn't an earthshaking event in the overall scheme of things, but the happenstance discovery of the uncanny similarities between these two photos on my hard drive struck me as being almost too good to be true.

14

Metaphor and Suggestion

You can't touch an intangible, but you can take its picture. Take a look at the content of this photo—only look beyond the visual of a vine wrapping itself around a rod of steel. See anything else? (Or maybe *see* is the wrong word: how about *perceive*?) Do you sense conveyances of harmony or co-existence? How about connotations of a different sort: strife or struggle? They're all there—all that's needed is a headline or perhaps some text to prompt the viewer toward certain conclusions.

Advertisers and designers often make use of metaphor-rich images such as this on book jackets and CD covers, and in magazine articles and ads.

I wandered across this scene of a vine coiling itself around a bar of steel outside a small outdoor shopping center. Fortunately, my car was parked nearby—and prepped for a day of picture-taking—so I was able to fetch my 50mm lens and capture a studio-quality, shallow depth-of-field shot. Later, I converted the photo to monochrome to further promote the image's quiet projection of mood.

238   239

The association between the vine and the metal bar in this image could be seen as a harmonious meeting of opposites. It could also be interpreted as a metaphor for struggle. Text could used to steer a photo like this in more than one thematic direction.

It's not hard to imagine a photo like this being used to accompany an article about nervous breakdowns or some other form of emotional distress. This type of photo is often used to augment—or take the place of—textual messages in advertising, design and literature. The prop used here, by the way, is a broken shish kabob skewer.

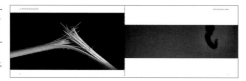

240   241

A photo of a heavy hook, hanging from the dimly lit ceiling of a warehouse delivers connotations of unease and fear. If you're thinking about building a collection of for-sale stock photos, images infused with metaphoric potential might make an especially good category to pursue. Train your eyes and mind to be on the lookout for material in day-to-day life. Keep a camera on hand, too: it's impossible to predict when you might cross paths with a metaphor.

And you thought you were having a bad day. On this spread, a couple of of busted-up mannequins deliver unmistakable conveyances of funk and distress.

242   243

Chance encounters with mannequins have led to many of my favorite photos. Luck was definitely smiling on me the morning when the photo on this page was taken. I came across this splendidly unkempt figure only a few blocks down the street from where I'd discovered the even more disjointed model seen on pages 339-340.

Few places on earth offer such a concentration of exquisitely-crafted sculptures as Florence and Rome—a good thing to keep in mind if you are interested in collecting images that are charged with splendid fabrications of human emotion.

244   245

When taking pictures of just about anything, consider framing the shot in a way that fills the composition with more open space than content. Also, think about tilting the camera so your subject enters the picture from a non-perpendicular angle. (And when it comes time to present the shot, how about about changing its impact completely by flipping the scene upside-down?)

Graphic symbols and words can be inserted into photos to boost existing connotations—and to add new ones. For instance, in the near image, illustrated bursts have been layered into the scene to increase the power lines' conveyances of energy; on the opposite page, mute photographs of loudspeakers have been given a visual voice through the addition of speaking bubbles and typographic symbols.

246

247

If speakers could speak, what would they say? And how would they say it? Where could you take the idea of adding "visual voices" to your own images of things? What kinds of messages would you be interested in conveying? Humorous? Poignant? Factual? Political?

In this spread's near image, a pair of brawny cogs mesh molars to generate industrial-strength conveyances of grit and strength. The photo's rugged thematic projections have been boosted by converting its colors to monochrome with a BLACK AND WHITE adjustment layer. CURVES controls were used to deepen the image's values and raise contrast levels.

248

249

Here, the sleek and tidy teeth of an entirely different specie of cog collaborate to produce connotations of sophistication and efficiency. Whatever message you're aiming to transmit through a photo, bolster it by treating the image to effects that echo and enforce the theme. This image was prettied with an aqua tint from a PHOTO FILTER treatment.

The cost of enlightenment? In this scene, a carved figure meditates peacefully in spite of the hefty price tag hanging from its neck.

250

251

The humiliation of renovation. A stately figure from Bernini's Fountain of the Four Rivers turns to peer from behind a construction screen (a related photo is featured on page 224). Ever travel in hopes of capturing beautiful images of a great work of art or architecture, only to find that your subject is being renovated or repaired when you get there? Don't despair (not totally, anyway) make the most of the situation by looking for photo opportunities of a different sort.

What's it all mean? I surely don't know, but it seemed like a no-brainer to fetch my camera when I came across this amazing mobile hanging from a tree in an outdoor second-hand market.

252

253

This shot was recorded using a 15mm fisheye lens. I had to stand on tiptoe and hold the lens far above my head while shooting. After each photo, I would lower the camera and check out the result on the LCD (it took several attempts before I started getting results I liked). I have nothing against cameras that use film, but I certainly appreciate being able to use a digital camera's LCD to review my images when circumstances force me to shoot willy-nilly.

15

Sign Language

Signs speak. And their visual voice is not only delivered through letters, numbers, words and symbols—it's also conveyed through the style, design, colors and condition of the signs themselves (apparently, the saying, "It's not what you say, but how you say it," doesn't only apply to humans).

Given this multi-level delivery of message and aesthetics, signs are especially valuable to photographers—not only as stand-alone subjects, but also for the conceptual and aesthetic boost they can lend to the scenes they inhabit.

A number of project ideas involving photos of signs are mentioned at the end of this chapter. Check them out if you're looking for more reasons than you already have to take pictures of this expressive and versatile category of subject matter.

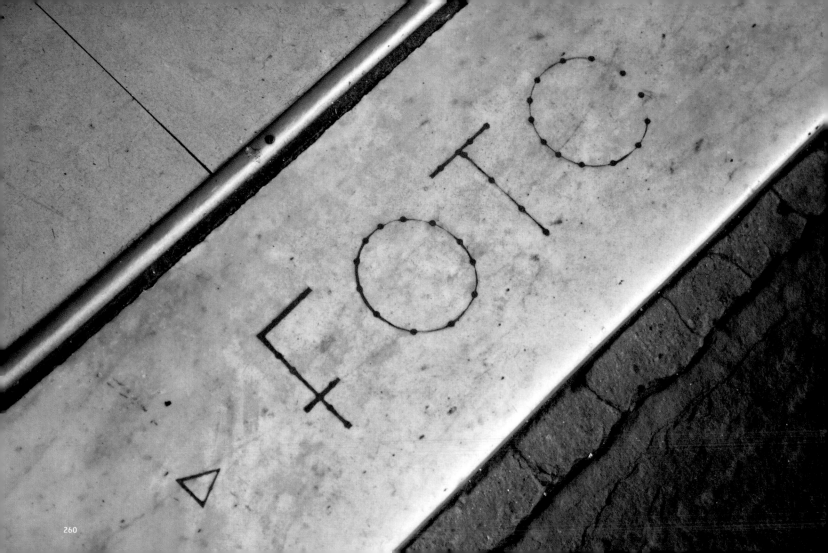

BARE FEET &
GH HEEL SHOES
RE DANGEROUS

ATCH FOR

ROCKS
KILL
FISH

What Can Be Done?

FASTEN SEAT BELT

IF YOU
NEED
ME CALL
229323

COOL BEER

NO
FOR OIL

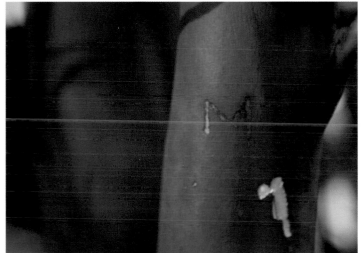

IN CASE OF DAMAGE OR
EMERGENCY PH 871-6200

DANGER
ELECTRICAL HAZARD
KEEP OUT

CONTI

267

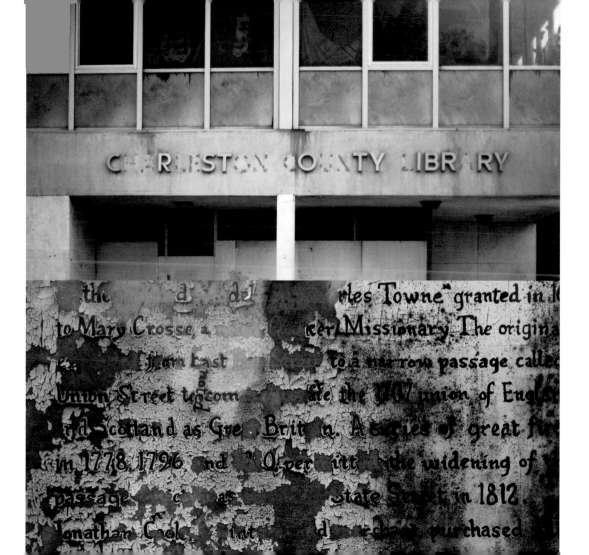

CHARLESTON COUNTY LIBRARY

the d de rles Towne" granted in 1

to Mary Crosse, a ker Missionary The origina

e rom East to a narrow passage calle

Union Street to com te the 1707 union of Engla

nd Scotland as Gre Brit n. A s ries of great f

in 1778, 1796 nd "O per itt the widening of

passage c as state S et in 1812

Jonathan C ob int d rch purchased

How often do you find yourself taking pictures of signs, numbers, letters, words and symbols? If your answer is *rarely* or *never*, it may be because you've never really felt there was much creative potential or value in this kind of subject matter. And if this is true for you, read on: Several project ideas are mentioned in the paragraphs ahead, and at least one of them may sway your opinion.

256

257

Who cares if it's just a traffic sign and a few clouds? Here, a pleasing mix of lines, curves, textures and colors amount to an appealing, ready-to-shoot subject and scene. Wondering what you might do with something like this—a photo of a sun-kissed traffic sign featuring a large numeral? Consider the ideas that follow.

A few things you can do with photos of numerals: Create a web or gallery show's worth of images that feature numbers 1 through 25 (50? 100?); use photos of numbers 1 through 10 as countdown-footage at the beginning of a homemade video; post a stock-image collection that contains only images of numbers; feature full-page photos of numbers to denote the beginning of each chapter in your next novel; prepare a month-long calendar using photos of numbers and give the calendar to a friend during their birthday month.

258

259

If your photos are ever used in works of design or advertising, make a point of framing certain subjects so that they are surrounded by large amounts of empty space. Why? Because photos like this leave plenty of room for the addition of a headline or a block of text.

More project ideas—this time using photos that contain words: Post a web gallery—or assemble a scrapbook—from your photographic collection of humorous, ironic and poignant textual messages; create a portrait of your hometown using only images of signs and graffiti; display an image with a purely textual message next to one whose pictorial content pairs well with it; print homemade greeting cards on an inkjet printer using photos that feature interesting messages from signage.

260

261

Once you've spotted a word or sentence you'd like to photograph (or anything else, for that matter) be sure to spend time looking for a vantage point that turns your finding into a full-fledged composition. Try out high points of view; low perspectives; straight-and-level framing; angled alignments.

Left: a pair of chrome tourist binoculars faces the sea in Charleston, South Carolina. Right: a hand-lettered message along the Sentiero del'Amore (Lover's Walk) in Italy's Cinque Terre. The light fixture in the far image was unlit in the photo's original version. When I viewed the un-altered original, I felt that the look of the dark fixture acted against the brighter sentiment written on the wall below. The bulb was "illuminated" by applying Photoshop's DODGE tool to the fixture and the area around it.

262

263

Do you write? Short stories? Long stories? Poetry? Lyrics? How about combining your know-how as a photographer with your literary skills? Here's one idea: Keep your eyes open for scenes containing words or short sentences and use these textual tidbits as titles for written pieces. Your image could be displayed alongside the written piece, used as a backdrop for the words, or printed as a cover for a hand-bound booklet that contains the story, poem or lyric.

A tattered Tibetan prayer flag hanging from a large oak blows in the breeze. The camera's lens (a 15mm fisheye) was held very near the foremost flag to allow its billowing form to fill the scene. A fast shutter speed (1/500th of a second) was selected so the fabric's threads and shreds could be photographed in crisp detail.

264   265

Be proactive: Take pictures of whatever initials and names you come across. That way, when a friend's birthday comes around, you stand as better chance of having what you need to create a clever and custom greeting card. As these two photos illustrate, I'm prepared to honor a friend whose name begins with "M," as well as a friend named "Amelia" (provided I ever happen to meet and befriend a person with that name).

Keeping in mind that I work as a graphic designer, can you guess which folder in my image browser holds more pictures than any other? If you guessed *flowers, sunsets, mountains, buildings* or *animals*, you guessed wrong. My most populated folder is *signs and symbols*. There are two reasons for this: first, the subject matter is everywhere, and second, in the design biz, there's never a shortage of potential uses for easily recognizable and conceptually-charged images of symbols.

266   267

Unless we are actively looking for a particular piece of information, our eyes and mind tend to overlook the signs and symbols that populate our environs. If you want proof of this, make a point of *trying* to notice every sign, symbol, poster, handbill and sample of graffiti you come across the next time you're in a bustling downtown district. You'll probably be amazed to see what you've been missing (both in terms of informational value and photo opportunities).

The last two spreads of this chapter feature images of signs whose official message is cryptic, broken or absent. Still, when looking at these images, you may feel (as I do) that the signs in the photos are not without something to say. Their dilapidated state speaks with surprising lucidity about the condition of their surroundings, the passage of time, and the effects of the elements.

268   269

Opposite page: Two signs that no longer contain messages (unless you count the clouds that can be seen when looking through the empty elliptical frame of one, or the abstract impression left by adhesive residue on the other). Near page: Two deteriorating signs that are losing their visual voice, letter by letter, word by word.

Near page: A solitary bicyclist pedals past a wall of washed-out posters and handbills. Opposite: Strips of peeling and sun-faded posters hang toward the camera. Both shots were taken in Lucca, Italy—a town whose narrow, high-walled streets provide an abundance of cool shadows and splendid reflected light for the comfort and enjoyment of camera-carrying tourists.

270   271

The contemporary, muted color scheme of these two photos was achieved by assigning the "screen" setting to the pull-down menu of a BLACK AND WHITE adjustment layer that had been added to each. After this was done, a PHOTO FILTER adjustment (set to "underwater") was added to each image.

16

Hidden Treasure

One person's trash is another's treasure, and *Beauty is in the eye of the beholder.*

If you accept the sentiment behind these familiar sayings—and have an interest in expanding your image portfolio—you're in luck: According the Environmental Protection Agency, the U.S. alone produces around 6 million tons of trash (or is that treasure?) each day.

Have doubts about your knack for turning garbage into gold? Take heart: A mindful and resourceful photographer has at least as good a chance of taking an attractive photograph of trash as an inattentive and hasty photographer has of taking a trashy photo of something beautiful.

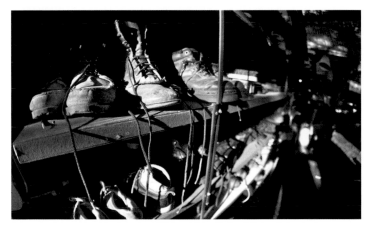

Tired of taking landscape photos? How about going after land*fill*-scapes instead? I chanced upon this massive pile of discarded tires at a racetrack in Spokane, Washington. The track was undergoing renovation and workers had spent weeks combing the grounds and the nearby sagebrush for garbage and piling it according to composition (metal, rubber, wood or miscellaneous). The tire pile was by far the largest.

274   275

One of the most surprising finds the clean-up crew made was a nearly intact 1950s Buick sedan that had been abandoned—who knows how long ago—behind a set of low hills just beyond the track's perimeter (the car is pictured on the spread below).

Left: The rising sun's rays have yet to reach the recovered hull of a 1959 Buick Electra sitting on a mat of scrubby desert grass. The colors in this shot have been amplified using Photoshop's HUE/SATURATION controls. Right: The hues in this image were muted using the sliders available in these same controls.

276   277

This van was one of two abandoned American vehicles I came across on the fringes of Belizian jungles during my visit to that country in 2007. I spotted both vehicles while riding in a rental car with two new-found friends from New York who had offered to show me some of their favorite hiking grounds in the area. They were a very considerate couple—kind enough to pull over whenever I spotted a must-have photo opportunity (and whether or not they agreed with my taste in subject matter).

Near page: A pair of discarded shoes hang from the bare branches of a tree. Opposite: A junked shopping cart carrying a disowned pair of jumper cables sits outside a vacated industrial site. Many photographers (myself included) enjoy the implication of an intriguing story line that so often accompanies scenes of abandonment.

278   279

Interested turning your photos of trash into treasure? How about turning your collection of desolate scenes and discarded things into a stock-image resource for designers? Commercial artists are well known for being able to use photos of this sort in magazine articles, on book covers and for music packaging.

Familiarity breeds connection. Viewers of the near photo might experience a certain measure of connection to the foreign environs pictured here simply because the scene contains an oh-so-familiar object: an empty beer bottle. The blurred row of bottles in the adjacent image (shot with an unsteady hand in the dim light of a nighttime alley) may also convey notes of familiarity to viewers who may have enjoyed one too many a time or two.

280   281

A semi-vintage soda pop cap (about 22 years old, according to the date printed on it) lies hammered into the top of a wooden pier in a Belizian bay. Though tiny, the cap's brilliant hue stood out shockingly against the supernaturally turquoise sea surrounding it.

On this spread the focus is on subjects of biological—rather than manufactured—origin. The pair of dead and drying leaves on the near page make interesting visual studies of texture and form. (More photos of lifeless plants can be found on pages 180-181.) The images were converted to monochrome using Photoshop's BLACK AND WHITE controls.

Near page: A struggling palm presides over a seaside pile of refuse along the Belizian coast. Meanwhile, halfway around the globe, the eyeless sockets of a skull mounted to a tall post keep watch over an Italian lemon orchard.

282   283

An up-for-grabs couch (along with a scattering of free-for-the-taking wardrobe items) sits in a back alley. If you spend much time looking at contemporary urban magazines, you've probably seen photos such as this—as true-to-life as they are ambiguous—used to accompany articles and essays. Being a fan of this type of scene, I make a point of taking the alley as often as possible when walking or biking through town.

What's making this mess? Are they monsters or miniatures? Here, an eye-fooling digital treatment has been used to cut a massive construction site down to size. The effect was created by using the LASSO tool to create a protective mask around the cranes' plane of perspective, and then using the blur tool to soften the focus elsewhere in the scene. (This effect can be also be achieved without the use of digital treatments by shooting with a "tilt-shift" lens.)

284   285

The kaleidoscopic mural on this spread was created by duplicating and mirroring a photo of a giant field of demolition refuse. The original photo was stretched in Photoshop and then given a blue tint with the PHOTO FILTER control prior to being cloned and reflected.

This multiple mirroring treatment is a favorite effect of mine. It's a very simple means of transforming a relatively mundane shot into an intriguing abstraction. I particularly enjoy applying the effect to industrial subjects, plant life and architectural details. How about looking through your image cache for shots that might be given a new artistic lease on life once treated in this way?

286   287

If you love second-hand stores as much as I do, and also enjoy taking pictures of unusual subject matter at least as much as me, you'll probably relate to the first thought that came into my head when I located this outdoor thrift market: *I've found paradise.*

Opposite page: A partial view of the market's sprawling array of goods and the trees that shelter them. Near page, clockwise from upper-left: Lamps of all shapes and sizes, crammed with care into a makeshift display room; a collection of orphaned chrome hubcaps; shelved shoes waiting patiently to be taken for walks by new pairs of feet; and a spring-horse, put to pasture (at least temporarily).

288   289

17

Inner Workings

What's behind the face of a clock? What does the brain of a computer look like? What kind of supports are needed to keep a bridge from falling down? In this chapter, screws are unfastened, appliances are dissected and journeys are made to the undersides of great structures to reveal—and photograph—the normally unseen workings of ordinary things.

If you are the curious type, and enjoy handling screwdrivers, wrenches and the occasional sledge hammer, you might especially enjoy going after photos like the ones featured ahead. Keep tabs on the wares of second-hand stores, garage sales and trash bins for the raw material needed to satisfy your inquisitive and creative urges.

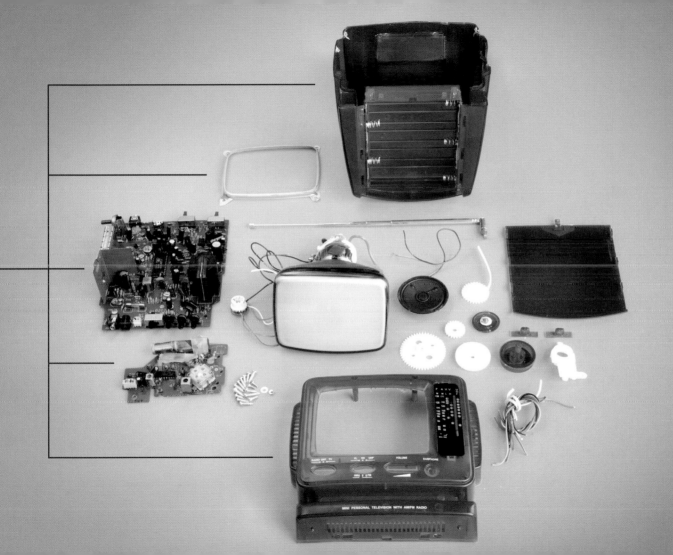

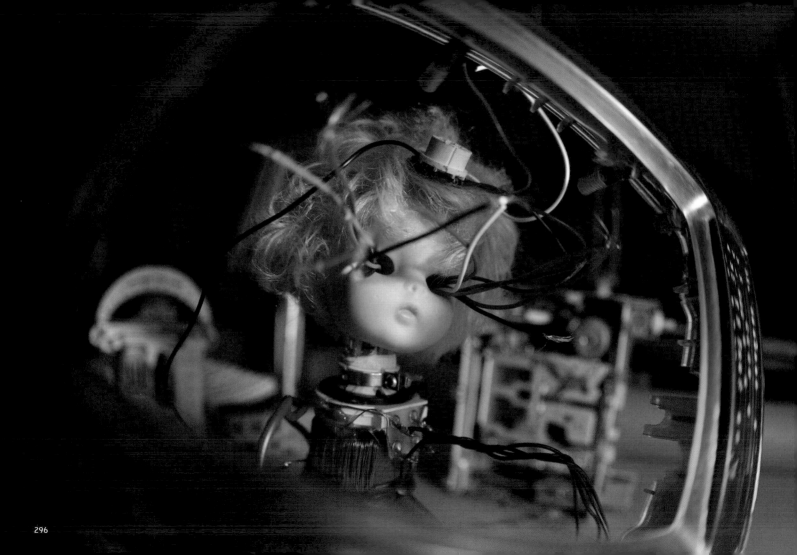

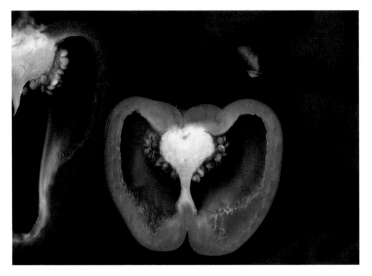

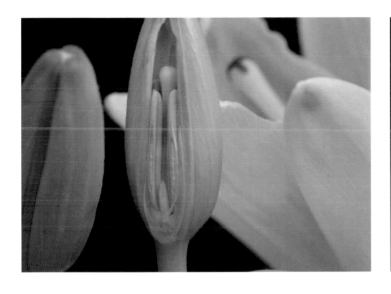

What's this? The insides of a multi-processor computer or a digital television? The guts of a data-storage unit? How about none of the above? This high-tech construction is make-believe. The image was built from a single photo of a circuit board. A duplicate of the original photo was altered using Photoshop's TRANSFORM > PERSPEC-TIVE tool and then repeated to form the "walls" around the original. HUE/SATURATION and CURVES adjustment layers were employed to color the composite image and to add the highlighted area at its center.

292

293

An illustration such as this has great pattern-building potential. Here, the composite original has been repeated two-and-a-third times. The original could just as easily have been shrunk and repeated hundreds of times to fill the spread.

Many of us grew up wondering how things worked and what was inside the mechanical toys and appliances around us. Using this chapter as an excuse, I purchased a mini-television from a thrift store, grabbed some screwdrivers, and took the thing apart. This spread features a before-and-after comparison of my efforts. The near image was removed from its background using the LASSO selection tool and then set against a white backdrop where the hint of a shadow was added using the AIRBRUSH tool.

294

295

A project idea: How about collecting some choice appliances from a second-hand store and photographing each before—and after—being broken down into its parts and pieces. A dozen or so pairs of photos of this kind could make for an interesting (not to mention, educational) showing on the web, in a gallery or on the walls of a cyber cafe.

Obey your creative impulses! After photographing the television's innards, I found myself with table full of wires, circuits, plastic bits and a cathode ray tube. It was then I happened to spy a doll's head sitting on a nearby shelf of props and decided it was time to quit working and to start creating. A short time later I had my franken-girl: part television and part doll (a creative out-come which, by the way, helps confirm my belief that televisions are much more valuable dead than alive).

296

297

How much color is enough? The answer, or course, depends on the mood and message you are hoping to project. HUE/SATURATION controls were used to boost the colors in the opposite photo, and also to mute the hues in the near image. Photoshop makes experi-mentation and alteration easy and fast. Spend time considering your options before deciding which look is right for any photo's ultimate presentation.

Few of the photos in this book were shot using what could really be considered a "studio" set up. These images, for instance, were taken by laying the subjects on my desk and lighting them with a bright desk lamp. The clock on the opposite page was set on a sheet of gold fabric prior to shooting. The images were recorded using an SLR fitted with a 50mm lens.

298

299

Novel images of common objects often appear in advertising and design where their conceptual conveyances could be used to emphasize a theme or message. Regular prop-shopping excursions to thrift stores are a good idea if you're interested in building a commercially viable collection of images based on everyday things like these.

I came across this cracked open television in the alley beneath an upper-story apartment (and from the looks of it, someone on the third floor feels the same way about TV as I do). Happenstance scenes such as this are yet another demonstration of my motivation to keep a camera on-hand at all times, *and* why I often choose to walk or ride my bike though back alleys instead of along major streets.

300

301

Wires crawl from the dash of a sadly decomposing VW bug. Both of the images on this spread would have looked good in black and white—though possibly more artistic than realistic. In this case, I decided to preserve the matter-of-fact realism of the scenes by leaving the colors as-shot.

Exposed conduits and a lit bulb hang from the ceiling of an auto ferry's mid-level deck. These shots were taken using the flexible focusing capabilities of a Lensbaby. This lens is small, easy to pack, and a lot of fun to use: I rarely leave it behind when I'm packing around a bag of lenses.

302

303

A change of scale. What about photographing the inner workings and undersides of things larger than gadgets, appliances and autos? Here, the dark metal beams of a railway bridge contrast sharply against the curved, reinforced concrete supports of the automobile overpass in the background.

Whether or not you consider yourself a food stylist, how about having a go at taking a few simple shots of the insides of some of your favorite fruits and vegetables? Subject matter could be as near as your refrigerator. The photo on the far left of the spread—like those featured on page 15—was recorded by setting the subjects on a flatbed desktop scanner.

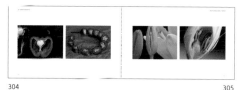

304

305

A sharp craft knife was used to expose the inner workings of these buds. If you have a particular interest in botanical wonders, how about creating a photo digest of both outer and inner details of some of your favorite specimens?

When it comes to taking pictures of the insides of things, it's always nice to come across a subject where someone else has done the work of peeling away its exterior surfaces. Here are a couple of images of an antique aircraft's wood-and-metal framework and controls. This wonderful display is housed in Seattle's Museum of Flight (more photos from this museum are featured in chapter 3, Components, pages 40-57).

306

307

Sometimes a photographer just gets lucky. I was scouting around the museum's old airplane hanger—looking for shots of the inner workings of actual airplanes—when I chanced across this detailed cut-away drawing of a 1940s aircraft.

18

Vehicles

Given their roles in the lives of humans worldwide, few (if any) inorganic objects can match the practical, emotional, social and cultural significance of cars, motorcycles, mopeds and bicycles.

And how readily available they are! Chances are, unless you live deep in the rain forest or near the top of a Himalayan peak, you have merely to step outside your home to catch sight of a wheeled vehicle of some kind or another.

Aesthetically, too, vehicles come in an alluring array of forms, configurations, colors and styles. This is all to say: cameras and wheeled conveyances are a match made in the heavens.

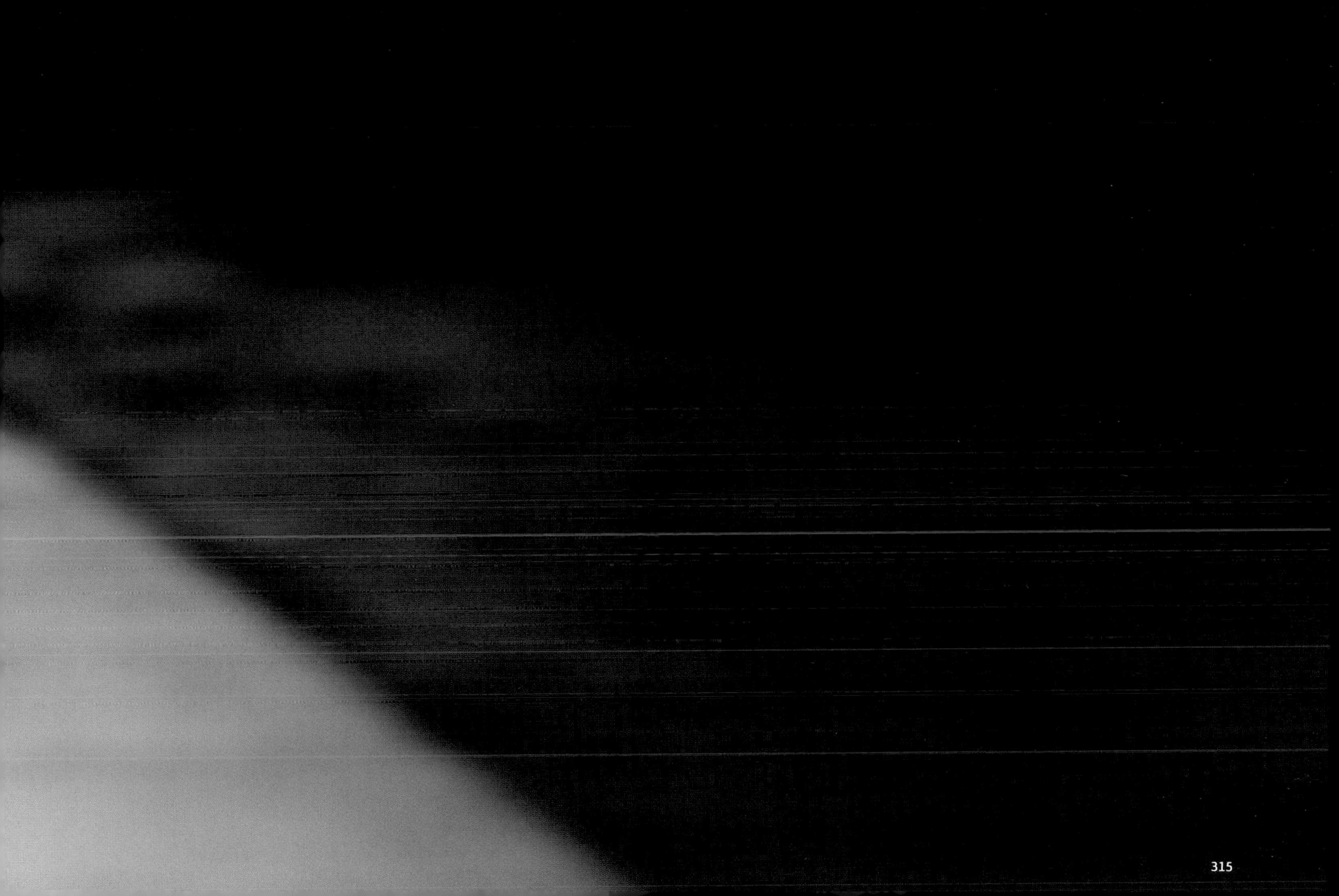

The first three shots in this chapter are from a series I've been working on called "Burn Out." The title serves as a reference to three aspects of the photos and their content: the heavily burned out (overexposed) nature of the photos; the act of burning out (spinning and smoking a car's tires) and also the emotional cultural burn-out society has experienced in terms of the giant, gas-gulping cars of the 1960s and 1970s.

310

311

Apart from religious icons, few common objects are as potently recognizable, as charged with emotional and social meaning, and allowed such supernatural status as the automobile. Here, with its wheels darkened nearly to the point of invisibility, the shimmering reverse-silhouette of this large 70s sedan almost appears to float above its asphalt parking spot.

A Lensbaby was used to capture this set of blurred and impressionistic images. The scenes were given a contrast-heightening treatment in Photoshop using a CURVES adjustment layer. HUE/SATURATION controls were employed to neutralize all but the scene's warmest hues.

312

313

The more common your subject matter, the more you may have to push yourself to find fresh and communicative ways of capturing its image. A few approaches worth considering: Take your pictures using an alternative lens such as a Lensbaby or pinhole; keep your eyes open for situations where your subject appears in an unlikely or humorous context; take your shot from an unusual or extreme perspective; apply exaggerated digital effects to your photo; or, all of the above.

How about doing everything wrong in hopes of coming up with a right photo? This photo, for example, conveys a communicative impression of time and place in spite of its blurred, overexposed, stretched and severely cropped content.

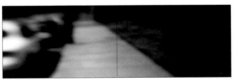

314

315

Once again: A reminder that photos that contain large areas of relatively content-free space make good candidates for graphic design projects where images and text are combined into layouts. The large expanse of uncluttered dark space on the right-hand side of this spread, for example, could easily be used to contain a light-colored headline and the first paragraph or two of text for a magazine article.

Passenger pictures. The next time you find yourself traveling as a passenger in an automobile, how about snapping a few photos? And how about aiming for shots that convey impressionistic glimpses of your journey (as opposed to tightly focused, highly descriptive images)?

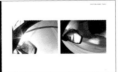

316

317

Each of the photos on this spread were taken with a 15mm fish-eye lens. The camera was set in "exposure priority" mode so that an exposure time could be found that introduced a measure of motion blur into the image. The camera was steadied by resting it against parts of the car's interior while shooting so that only the moving elements in the scene outside the car would be blurred.

Motorcycles and mopeds are as much a part of Italian culture as cappuccinos and football (a.k.a. soccer). Being a fan of two-wheeled vehicles myself, I devoted a serious amount of memory-card space to images of these machines (and their replicas) during a two-week visit to Rome and Florence. Near page, left: a pair of miniatures stand parked in a merchant's window display. Right: a colorful trio of mosaics hang above the tail end of a block-long row of mopeds and motorcycles. Opposite: A no-cars-allowed parking lot.

318

319

Morning in Rome: The workday awakens and mopeds and motorcycles begin to disappear from their overnight parking spaces. This shot was taken from a low vantage point using a 12-24mm wide angle lens. Photoshop's BLACK AND WHITE controls were used to convert the image to monochrome and to encourage the inclusion of some digital noise (a look that helps convey some of the scene's urban edginess). A CURVES adjustment layer was also applied to boost the photo's contrast.

A man and his motorcycle. Don't forget the value of including people in your photos of things. Here's a project idea: take a portrait of each of your closest friends while they sit in or on a favorite car, motorcycle, moped or bike. Then, how about putting all the images on display in your home and having the participants come over to raise a toast to the photos—and to each other?

320

321

I was thrilled to to arrive at my friend's house to find his front yard riddled with the remains of the previous night's snowfall. What amazing visual texture it lent to the scene. And since I couldn't decide which version of the photo I liked better—monochrome or color—I decided to feature both here. (Sharp-eyed viewers may have already noticed that the motorcycle's logo and the house's address were digitally flipped when the image was mirrored.)

Being a proponent of bicycling, I was inspired by the abundance and variety of bikes I came across in Italy. Rare was the street, alley or sidewalk that didn't have between one and a hundred bikes parked along its length—everything from rusty old utilitarian models to well-kept classic cruisers to sleek carbon-fiber racers.

322

323

This streetside scene has been given a radical makeover using a simple Photoshop treatment: the GRADIENT MAP effect. Add this effect as an adjustment layer (rather than applying it directly to the image). This way, you can easily explore variations in how the effect is applied—and can freely change your mind- until the image is flattened for presentation.

The photographs on this spread were taken during evening races (another photo from this event is featured on pages 154-155). The light was dim and the borrowed lens I had with me couldn't take in enough light to capture crisp photos of the action. This turned out to be an okay thing: The blurred images that resulted feature intriguing and descriptive conveyances of speed—conveyances that may have been lost if the photos had been shot in a more technically refined manner.

324

325

Advice: Strive to gain a thorough understanding of how your camera works. Make an effort to comprehend the rules of "proper" photography (that is, perfectly exposed images, crisply focused content, and so on). And, at the same time, nurture the creative instincts that tell you when to break these rules in pursuit of interesting and attractive images. Those who know the rules best are often those who how to break them best.

19

Art, Out and About

Cameras are a unique creative medium in that they can be used to create one's own art, *and* to capture the art of others. In this, the final chapter of **Photo Idea Index: Things**, the lens is trained on the creations of others—with a special emphasis on the spontaneously occurring types of art that occur outside the confines of galleries or exhibits.

Sculptures, assemblages, paintings and graffiti can be found wherever people live, work, hang out and play. Keep your eyes open for these ready-to-photograph artistic expressions. And when you decide to take a picture of one of your findings, aim to multiply its visual offerings by capturing an image that boosts the aesthetic and conceptual conveyances of your subject.

WINTER
IS
HERE.

Improvisation and art: It's all spelled out in this photo. (This is the exterior of the office at the outdoor second-hand market whose images are featured on pages 288-289.) The fisheye lens used to capture this photo adds a relevant note of curvaceous animation to the image.

328   329

When I came upon this scene, I knew right away I'd found the opening photo for this chapter. With this in mind, I intentionally aimed for content that would fit into the extreme horizontal format needed for this spread. I'd already placed a couple small pieces of tape on my camera's LCD that indicate the proper proportions needed for this cropping—a very helpful aid. Consider doing something similar if you are regularly seeking a cropping that's significantly different from your camera's default image proportions.

There's something about a beach that seems more capable of prompting creative expression than most other environments. Who knows who built this clever design of piled stones—it was simply left behind by an earlier beach-goer for later visitors to enjoy and photograph.

330   331

This page, left photo: the anonymous person who stuck these bare branches into the sand may or may not have had artistic goals in mind when they did it. Still, I thought the sticks presented an aesthetically commanding photo opportunity. At right: I was walking along a bayside path close to my home when I happened across a man painstakingly balancing these large and mid-sized rocks (and yes, the rocks really are balancing upon each other without any artificial aids—no glue, no chewing gum, no nothing).

Last winter, some thoughtful and anonymous donor knitted turtleneck scarves for several downtown trees—a sight that brought out smiles (and cameras) from passersby all winter long.

332   333

I chanced upon this makeshift testament to the holidays while walking along the barbed-wire fence around a deserted industrial site. "Winter is here" is the inscription on the cup stuck into the fence at lower right—a sentiment that seemed more melancholy than joyful given the frigid bleakness of the day and the shrine's surroundings. (The abandoned shopping cart featured on page 279 was photographed just a few feet from from this scene).

Here's another lucky shot. I was taking a picture of this artfully constructed mailbox—in fact I was already kneeling down with my eye to the viewfinder and my finger on the shutter button—when this beautiful classic sedan rolled into the frame. I kid you not. I guess it's like anything else: if you spend enough time doing something (taking pictures, in this case), you're bound to have your share of lucky accidents along the way.

334   335

Here's a view of the same road, and the same residence/kayak rental shop, only the camera is facing the opposite direction. Both of these images were converted to tinted monochromes using Photoshop's BLACK AND WHITE controls. A slightly different tint was applied to each for the sake of creating a note of individuality between them.

I've never been one to decorate public spaces with spray paint and stencils, but I've always enjoyed taking pictures of work of people who do. Graffiti: if you can't beat it, you might as well take pictures of the better stuff.

336

337

The eyes of a faithfully reproduced Renaissance portrait peers from a mural pasted onto a construction facade. A crowd in the background mills around the entrance to the spectacular Uffizi gallery in Florence.

I spotted this decorated window case just after getting off the freeway on my first-ever visit to Charleston, South Carolina. The next morning, bright and early, I returned to the scene because I knew it was find of rare artistic value and worth. The morning sun did a wonderful job of illuminating the display in flattering light.

338

339

The tilted framing of this shot bolsters the animated and quirky conveyances of the scene. Many photographers resist tilting their camera when shooting horizontal subject matter—apparently, there's just something about the practice that feels wrong to some people. If you're a perpetually straight-and-level shooter, loosen up and take that off-kilter shot every once in a while. You might like the results and you might not—but at least you'll be pushing the creative envelope.

This spread features images of a couple pseudo shrines I keep on shelves in my office. These assemblages change continuously—depending on my mood, how much spare time I have, and whether or not I have any new collectibles to add to the mix. Do you collect pieces of memorabilia? If so, how about putting together a few groupings and snapping some photos? An additional thought: what if you were to take the same set of elements and create—and photograph—a dozen different arrangements of them?

340

341

These collections of objects sit inside shelves that measure only about 12 inches high, wide and deep. The photos were captured by holding a 15mm fisheye lens at the shelves' openings. The far image was taken using natural light; a flashlight was used to illuminate the near scene. For the final presentation, the shots were converted to monochrome and given a blue-green tint with a PHOTO FILTER adjustment. Digital noise was added to the images with the NOISE > ADD NOISE effect.

A large hanging metal sculpture coils in the breeze beneath a canopy of tall trees. This sculpture was created by Anthony Howe, an artist who lives and works on Orcas Island in Washington state. Mr. Howe has long been kind enough to hang some of his beautiful works of art from roadside trees for others to enjoy.

342

343

The clever creations of a talented builder of bird homes adorn a line of fence posts (in fact, this entire property was ringed by colorful birdhouses—each one different from the next). The image was snapped with a 75-200mm telephoto lens, zoomed-in from a vantage point that allowed me to fit as many of the birdhouses into the frame as possible.

Glossary

Note: Any Photoshop controls, functions or tools are denoted by the use of SMALL CAPS.

ADJUSTMENT LAYER. A layer added to an image in Photoshop to alter characteristics such as contrast, levels and color balance. Alterations made using an ADJUSTMENT LAYER can be revised by double-clicking on it in the LAYERS palette and readjusting its controls (an option that would not be available if the original adjustments had been applied directly to the image using a menu command). ADJUSTMENT LAYERS can also be selectively applied to an image. This is done by using the PAINTBRUSH or other rendering tools to create regions of varying opacity in the MASK layer that automatically accompanies an ADJUSTMENT LAYER when it is created. Consult Photoshop's help menu or manual for detailed information about these useful and easy to use image editing tools.

Aperture. The adjustable iris-like opening inside a lens that controls how much light reaches the image sensor. Some cameras allow for manual control of the aperture opening—others handle its functions automatically. Aperture affects both exposure and depth-of-field.

Backlighting. A lighting arrangement where the subject is between the camera and the light source.

Bracketing. A technique of taking a set of photos—each shot at a slightly different exposure—to help ensure that at least one is properly exposed. Most brackets are shot in sets of three images. Full-featured digital cameras usually offer an automatic bracketing feature that shoots a burst of three differently exposed shots when the shutter button is pressed.

CHANNEL MIXER. An editing tool in Photoshop that allows the user to adjust the distribution of red, green and blue in an image. These color channels can also be isolated—by selecting the CHANNEL MIXER's "monochrome" option—as a way of converting an image to black and white.

CMYK. Abbreviation for cyan, magenta, yellow and black. For most printing purposes, images need to be converted from their native RBG mode to CMYK via software.

Continuous shooting mode. A feature of many digital cameras that allow them to take a steady stream of shots while the shutter button is held down.

Crop. To select only a desired portion of an image for display.

CURVES. A highly adjustable Photoshop control that allows the user to control the distribution of values and hues within an image.

Depth-of-field. The zone in which the camera sees things as being in focus. Objects outside this zone (both nearer to and further from the camera) appear out of focus. Depth-of-field is the product of several factors:

the focal length of the lens being used; the distance to the object being focused on; and the aperture opening (a narrower opening means a deeper depth-of-field; a wider opening means a shallower depth-of-field).

Desaturate. The removal of all color hues from an image. Full desaturation results in a black and white image.

Exposure. The amount of light that reaches the image-sensor to create an image.

Fisheye lens. A lens with an extremely wide field of view—from 100° to 180° and beyond.

Framing. A visual term used to describe when certain elements of a composition enclose others.

Grayscale image. Another term for a black and white image.

Hue. Another term for color.

HUE AND SATURATION. A control within Photoshop that allows for adjustments to the color, intensity and brightness qualities of a specific hue—or all hues globally—within an image. These adjustments can be applied directly to an image throush a menu command or through an adjustment layer.

LASSO TOOLS. A family of tools within Photoshop that are used to manually select elements with clipping paths.

LCD. Liquid Crystal Display. A panel on the back of most digital cameras that can be as a viewfinder, to review images, and to control menu items.

LEVELS. A control within Photoshop that allows adjustments to be made to an image's range of values and color balance.

Macro lens. A lens specifically designed to take close-up photos. Most macro lenses have a magnification ratio of 1:1 or greater.

Monochromatic. An image or scene composed of values of one hue.

Overexposure. The effect that occurs when cells of the image sensor receive so much light that the corresponding areas of the image are pure white. Some photographers consider overexposure unacceptable in images—others allow it for visual or thematic effect.

Pixel. A single cell within the complex grid of individual hues that make up an image captured by a digital camera.

Resolution. The level of detail recorded by a digital camera. Also the level of detail present in an on-screen or printed image.

RGB. Red, green and blue: The three colors with which digital cameras and computer monitors build their images. Images in RGB format can be converted to other color models (such as CMYK) using software.

Saturation. The intensity of a hue. Highly saturated colors are at their most intense. Colors with low levels of saturation appear muted.

SHADOW/HIGHLIGHT. A control within Photoshop that allows the user to bring out details within overly dark or overly light areas of an image.

Shutter speed. The duration of time during which the shutter is open (and thereby allowing light to reach the image sensor) during a shot.

SLR. Single Lens Reflex. A camera whose viewfinder sees through the same lens that will be sending light to the image-sensor. The lenses on most SLRs are interchangeable.

Standard zoom lens. A versatile lens that has a field of view comparable to the human eye's central viewing area. This lens is also capable of moderate image magnification.

Telephoto lens. A relatively compact lens capable of a wide range of telescopic magnifications.

Underexposure. The effect that occurs when cells of the image sensor have not received enough light to fully portray the corresponding areas of an image.

Value. the relative lightness or darkness of a color or shade compared to a scale of white to black.

Visual texture. A dense repetition of elements that form anything from an organized pattern to a freeform, chaotic assemblage.

White balance. The way in which a camera measures and records prevailing light so that whites—as well as all other colors—appear normal to the eye of the viewer.

Wide-angle lens. A lens with a broad field of view.

The following is a list of the cameras and lenses
used for this book's images.

CAMERAS:
Canon 5d
Canon 20d
Canon S5IS
Canon SD500

A Canon LiDI30 desktop scanner was also used to record three of the book's images.

LENSES:
Canon 50mm 1:1.4
Canon 15mm 1:2.8 Fisheye
Canon 100mm 1:2.8 Macro
Canon 24-105mm 1:4
Sigma 12-24mm 1:4.5-5.6
Canon 70-200mm 1:2.8
Lensbaby Muse
Custom-made pinhole

Sample images from this
book's companion volume,
Photo Idea Index: Places

More Great Titles from Jim Krause and HOW Books!

Photo Idea Index: Places

In *Photo Idea Index: Places*, Jim Krause shows you how to use your camera to explore the world around you from different perspectives and how to capture awe-inspiring digital images. Learn new shooting techniques—both on-site and post-shooting digital treatments—so you can train your eyes to look for unique shots and remarkable compositions.

#z1590, 360 pages, paperback, ISBN: 978-1-60061-043-1

Complete Color Index

With over 2,600 color combinations, this box set is all you'll need for color inspiration! It contains the original best-selling *Color Index* and *Color Index 2*, and together they comprise the most comprehensive color selection tool out there. Each color palette has RGB and CMYK combinations, so you'll always be able to choose the perfect color combination for your project.

#z2976, 720 pages total, vinyl paperbacks in box, ISBN: 978-1-60061-333-3

Design Essentials Index

Combining three invaluable, practical design books for idea-hungry designers, *Design Essentials Index* offers everything from new color-combination systems to an in-depth examination of practical applications of type. This box set includes Jim Krause's best-selling *Design Basics Index*, *Type Idea Index* and *Color Index 2* to give designers a wealth of practical design information.

#z2375, vinyl paperbacks in box, ISBN: 978-1-60061-142-1

Photo Idea Index

Photo Idea Index is the original inspirational guide to taking creative photographs, exploring different digital manipulations, and using them in real-world design applications. Full of thought-provoking suggestions for broadening your range of photo skills, this book is a must-have for everyone, from the beginner to the accomplished photographer.

#33435, 360 pages, vinyl paperback, ISBN: 978-1-58180-766-0

HOW BOOKS

Find these and other fine HOW Books titles at your local bookstore or www.howbookstore.com.